INSPIRING & SOUL LIFTING BIBLE VERSES

120 DEVOTIONALS FOR MEDITATION WITH PRAYER POINTS

GIDEON O. OJO

i

This Book

is a

Special Gift

From

____

To

____

Date

____

Inspiring
& Soul Lifting
BIBLE VERSES

120 DEVOTIONALS FOR MEDITATION WITH PRAYER POINTS

GIDEON O. OJO

INSPIRING & SOUL LIFTING BIBLE VERSES
(120 DEVOTIONALS FOR MEDITATION
WITH PRAYER POINTS)

OTHER BOOKS BY THE SAME AUTHOR

THE CHAMPION IN YOU

FAITH CAPSULES

TOUCHED BY LOVE FOREVER

10 THINGS GOD EXPECTS FROM YOU

120 PROMISES OF GOD

PATHWAY TO EFFECTIVE PRAYER

Dedication

I thank Christ Jesus our Lord
who has given me strength,
that he considered me trustworthy,
appointing me to his service.
1 Timothy 1:12 (NIV)

To every reader whose life will be
transformed
To have a better and good relationship
in walking with GOD.

 INTRODUCTION

Each new day provides you with the privilege to meet with new friends, encounter new opportunities, develop new habits, start afresh, enjoy a new life, and bring you into new challenges. Of course, life was never designed to be challenges-free, because if it were, no one would ever outgrow their past, thereby repeating a vicious cycle of absolute limitation and stagnancy.

It is in hard times you learn new things; different from the norms, which helps you change and become a better version of yourself. The truth of the matter is challenges are inevitable; it is part of human life. But, how do you cope with life challenges when you encounter one? Do you go through the rituals of being depressed, angry, and frustrated, while you expect the situation to change itself? Or do you make plans on ways out of your challenges?

Now, there are a lot of human theories, philosophies, and ideologies as regards ways to handle life situations and control the things that happen around your life. These human perspectives on solving life problems seem good and palatable. However, none of it is as potent as God's provision through His word- THE BIBLE.

The Bible is the surest way out of any circumstances or condition that seems to threaten your peace, happiness, and fulfillment in life. The Bible is littered with words of wisdom and insight that can help you live a victorious life.

Do you feel helpless and hopeless? Are you in a toxic relationship and do not know a way out of it? Are you going through hard times? Are you at the edge of your life, and it seems everything you had ever worked for is at the verge of collapsing? Well, never lose heart yet.

This book is a compilation of one hundred and twenty (120) profound bible verses, full of wisdom, inspiration, instruction, and the very heartbeat of God for you. You will find hope, faith, strength, encouragement, and beauty as you walk through each page of this book.

Day 1

THE MOUNTAINS MELT
LIKE WAX (PART ONE)

---

*"The mountains melt like wax at the presence
of the LORD, at the presence of the Lord of
the whole earth."-Psalm 97:5*

One thing you must be aware of today is that the mountains do not disappear, they melt. They do not disappear into the thin air, they melt! Again, the mountains do not melt anyhow, but like wax. How does wax melt? It is by being subjected to heat. This means that your mountains are first subjected to heat before they begin to melt.

A very good example is candle wax. You have to kindle some fire on the thread and leave it until the flame begins to heat the wax and it melts. There are two major factors for the wax to melt: heat and time. The Bible says the mountains melt like wax which signifies the ease and the process. Mountains are strong and rigid and would need dynamites to break some parts of them but all these struggles only belong to men; not God. With God, mountains are handled like wax. What you spend restless days and sleepless nights to solve only needs a touch from God to melt away. Can you see where you have given the problem a means to boast? When the LORD comes, they are treated as simple as wax.

Nevertheless, you need fire--the fire of the Holy Ghost to put your troubles in bigger trouble; that will shake their foundation and force them to reduce until they are nowhere to be found.

Whenever the Lord descends on your mountains, fire comes on them and they have to begin to melt away. In Exodus 19:18, the Bible says:

"Now Mount Sinai was completely in smoke because the LORD descended upon it in a fire. Its smoke ascended like the smoke of a furnace, and the whole mountain quaked greatly"

Can you see how mountains can quake at the presence of the LORD your God? When you introduce the LORD to the mountain challenging you right now, the fire from Heaven will descend and cause that mountain to begin to melt away. You get this fire in prayers. Look up to God today for fire from above that will deal with all the mountains and hills.

PRAYER POINT:
LORD God, you are the consuming fire that melts every mountain in my way. I call upon you this day to come with your fire and set all the mountains that have withstood me these days on fire and they begin to melt in Jesus's name.

$\mathcal{D}ay\,2$

THE MOUNTAIN MELT LIKE WAX (PART TWO)

"The mountains will melt under Him, and the valleys will split like wax before the fire, like waters poured down a steep place" -Micah 1:4

As you have understood that what deals with mountains is the fire of the LORD and that the fire of His presence melts the mountain, you must also know that it takes time to melt away. In the natural, melting of a solid matter takes place over a period of time as the temperature of its molecules rises, breaking the bonds that were kept rigid before. Likewise, in the spiritual, mountains take time to melt. Take water, for example, it has three states, namely Ice (solid), water (Liquid), and vapor (gas). When sufficient heat is applied to ice, it begins to melt until it completely becomes liquid and it flows; when more heat is applied, the liquid begins to vapourize. But all of these processes take time to happen. They don't happen in a second. Similarly, wax melts under heat until it begins to flow like water.

Not every challenge melts away overnight. Some take minutes, some hours, some days, some weeks, some months, and other years. But they will surely melt away like wax. That you are not seeing the obvious result of your prayers now does not mean nothing is happening. Each time you apply heat to the wax, it melts-gradually. Put pressure on the devil and he will eventually flee from you. Heat the demons troubling your dreams and stopping your visions and they will melt away with time.

Keep adding more and more fire until you see the giant mountains become flowing water. You wonder how can mountains become water? That is the operation of the Presence of God. When He comes upon the mountain in fire, the heating begins, and gradually the mountains melt away and flow down like water until they cannot be called a mountain anymore.

Allow the process of melting in your life. Don't give up because you have not seen the appearance. Something is changing. The mountains are melting. The fire is building up and the ways are opening. Keep praying and you will see the whole thing reduce to nothing before you.

PRAYER POINT:

I thank you Father for this assurance of your work in my life. Now I know something is changing in my life even if it appears not yet. I will not give up on you. I will not stop praying until all mountains melt away and flow down like fire under your feet. Only give me the grace to watch and pray until it is finished. In Jesus's name, I pray. Amen.

Day 3

PEACE! BE STILL

"Then He arose and rebuked the wind and said to the sea "Peace, be still!" And the wind ceased, and there was a great calm" - Mark 4:39-40

Glory to God! Nothing can withstand the presence of God. Mountains melt at his presence. Rocks skip like rams at his appearance, even the sea and the ocean obey Him when He speaks. This is the God you serve. He is mighty in all and through all. His words become laws, and his decrees are actions. When He speaks, nothing can resist his voice. Surely, God will speak to every storm of your life today.

Life can feel like turbulence, chaotic, with various troubles. Your challenges, no matter how enormous it could be, can never be bigger than God. If God is for you, who can be against you? No one. Your life troubles are not permitted when you allow God to take over the wheel of your life. He is the God of all peace, and in Him, you will find perfect peace, completeness, and wholeness.

Running from challenges can never keep you from it because they will inevitably rise. Life will throw pebbles along your smooth path. People will rise against you. They will hate you. Those that you once trust will deny you and your strength will fail you when you need it the most. But in the midst of it all, always remember you have God, who is the prince of peace.

God sent Jesus as the prince of peace to give you peace in the troubled world. When you embrace Jesus, then you allow peace into your life. He will provide you with peace, even amidst that toughest situation. He will grant you safety even in that journey. He will keep your heart in perfect peace, regardless of how challenging that project might be. Today, I want you to embrace Jesus as he walks you through all life trouble and bring you to safety.

PRAYER POINT

Father, I pray that you speak peace into every turbulent situation of my life. I ask that you come and dwell in my heart, in my home, and my life forever.

$\mathcal{D}ay\,4$

HE GIVES STRENGTH TO THE WEARY

"He gives power to the weak, and to those who have no might, He increases strength." - Isaiah 40:29

Are you on the verge of giving up? Do you feel like you cannot continue anymore? Are you tired, and you want to quit? Please, hold on! Before you call it quit, I will like you to read further.

Weakness is a part of human makeup that cannot be denied. The strongest of us will eventually get weak - the toughest fails. The young ones among us never do much before they quit. Why do people feel this way? Well, people get tired and back out when they try but no result to show forth.

Surely, if you can allow God on your project and you can give him all that you have, he will provide you with all you need for life. God provides strength in exchange for human weakness. He gives power to the powerless and the helpless;

He renders a hand of help. You need to stop holding onto what cannot take you through life for long.

Your strength will fail you, but God will never. Your qualification, academic prowess, skills, and talent are not enough where more is needed from you. The truth of the matter is that you cannot give more than you have. However, when you give God what you have, He will surely give you what you lack.

There is no more insufficiency in your life henceforth. No more weakness because the almighty God is set to give you strength abundantly. Hence, do not look at what you lack, but focus on what God can give you. Stop complaining. Instead, I want you to embrace God's provision. Rejoice in what He had made available for you in Christ Jesus. Through Christ, you have it all.

PRAYER POINT

Father Lord, I give you my all. Take all of me and give me you. I receive the strength of God today.

$\mathcal{D}ay\,5$

GOD'S WORD ILLUMINATES

***"Your word is a lamp to my feet and a light
to my path." -Psalms 119:105***

Have you ever tried to walk in the dark before? The story most times does not have a good end, as you end up hitting your legs and head against walls. Now, to walk in the dark without light is walking into danger. How do you plan to know your way out of a dark environment without traces of light?

Similarly, the word of God is a light that lightens the way for believers. Without this light, there is no direction or destination. How frequent are you with God's word? Is it once, twice, or three times a month or year, maybe not at all?

You see, many at times believers complain not to hear God as though it is God's fault. You cannot hear God if you do not hear his word. God speaks expressly to your heart if only you have read what is in the bible. Consequently, do not confuse God's word for the bible. In the bible, men spoke, even the serpent spoke. The bible is not the word of God but in the bible, you will find the words of God.

Always create a habit of searching the words of God in the bible for in it are instruction for your life, light for your dark path, and revelations for victorious living. God's word directs. His words lead. The word of God encourages. It gives strength in times of temptation. It tells you what to do at every point in life. Learn to always turn to God through his words anytime you need light and illumination for your life.

PRAYER POINT:
Father your word is the light that shows the way. Help me to read, study, and meditate on your word as often as I should so that I will not be lost.

Day 6

THE LORD WILL DEFEND YOU

"The LORD shall fight for you, and ye shall hold your peace" - Exodus 14:14

The battle of life can be so fearsome that you will feel the end has already come. You have tried seeking help where it cannot be found. There is no better help you need than God. They call Him the mighty man in battle who has never lost one. Anyone with God is more than a billion.

"There shall no evil befall thee, neither shall any plague come nigh thy dwelling. For he shall give his angels charge over thee, to keep thee in all thy ways. They shall bear thee up in their hands, lest thou dash thy foot against a stone. Thou shalt tread upon the lion and adder: the young lion and the dragon shalt thou trample under feet." (Psalms 91:10-13)

A battle can be anything that takes away your peace, joy, or happiness, which might be family issues, challenges at the place of work, a frustrating boss, assault from haters, or every other thing that gives you no reason for living.

Battles are what we encounter daily, which most times are beyond our sphere of control.

Dear friend, all you need to do is surrender your life to Him. Battles will undoubtedly come, and you cannot fight them alone. You need a greater force to help you. Cast all your fears and problems on Him, and He will fight for you.

PRAYER POINT:
Lord Jesus, I surrender all my fears and battles before you today, come and fight for me in Jesus' name. Thank You, Father, in Jesus' name I have prayed.

Day 7

THE CARE THAT PRESERVES

"You have granted me life and favor, and your care has preserved my spirit." -Job 10:12

The word preserved is from the Hebrew word 'Shamar', and it means to guard, keep, protect, watch over, care for, and safe keep. The word occurs more than 400 times in the Old Testament alone. Its first usage can be traced back to Gen 2:15 when God told Adam to guard Eden. God is not just interested in giving you life and favor alone. He also wants to use His care to preserve your spirit, soul, and body. His name is called "Shomer Yisrael" which means the one who guards Israel. He is so committed to you so much more that He does not sleep nor slumber on His duty preserving you. No one else can shower on you the kind of care that He freely gives. This should continuously make you happy, no matter what you physically experience.

Some friends could have won your trust because of consistency, punctuality, and reliability. You could trust their judgment without a second thought. God is surer than the highest measure of strength displayed by any man. He has never failed, and He won't start it now. His care is stronger to preserve and keep you. Rejoice, you have life and favor from God and also, surer care that can preserve and guard you through life circumstances.

To care is to pay close attention to, to show concern, and be responsible for something or someone. Nothing gladdens a man's heart than knowing that someone cares for him. God cares about you so much. You must be fully persuaded of this that even His silence is a sign that He is working. God's silence when Jesus was on the cross eventually led to Christ sitting on a throne higher than every named throne.

Has he been silent for a while? Does it look like your prayer is without response yet? Then He is busy working things out. This is the acknowledgment of God's promises in your life. It takes one thing for the promise to be fulfilled, and it takes another for you to acknowledge it. Even if no one else cares about you, your heavenly Father does, and His care will preserve you till the end of days.

PRAYER POINT:
I walk in abundant life and favor of God today and always. God's care preserves me from all odd. I have a goodly heritage.

Day 8

THE WORKING FAITH!

"So Jesus answered and said to them, "Assuredly, I say to you, if you have faith and do not doubt, you will not only do what was done to the fig tree but also say to this mountain, 'Be removed and cast into the sea, it will be done." -Matthew 21:21

Just imagine what faith can do, this is a promise of great exploits! '…you will not only do what was done to the fig tree but also say to this mountain, be removed and cast into the sea…'

Take this mountain as a problem that has taken the best part of you; maybe, financial difficulties, health-related issues, breakdown of an epidemic disease, marital conflict, family problems, barrenness, you just name it. God has paved the way for us, a way that Faith leads to, and this way is the solution to every mountain (problems) in your life. You might wonder how this is possible, and if it can be done. Yes, it can if you just simply believe and have faith.

God has assured us of hope and breakthrough; He has deposited in you the power to do great exploits, take charge, and you don't even know it, why? You've allowed the Devil to step in and have a hold. The Devil has created a system that he continually uses to control the lives of people, and it is time you shake yourself off that system, which is FEAR.

FEAR, Fake Evidence Appearing Real. It shakes, mocks, and makes jest of the Faith you have in God the moment you let it take over you. It is prominent you know that Faith is a thing of belief, Hebrew 11: 1 says, "Now, faith is the substance of things hoped for, the evidence of things not seen." You believe even when you do not see the light at the end of the tunnel, you believe the evidence and assurance that every mountain in your life is cast away, you even believe when hope seems to fade off, that is Faith!

There is no problem that is too big for God. Know that He would never give you too much than you can handle. So, when trials come, and everything seems to be going wrong, remember that you have a God that has promised you great things. This God doesn't want you to give way to fear and doubts.

So, stand firm in your faith and be ready to remove and cast a mountain into the sea!

PRAYER POINT:
Heavenly Father, I strongly hold unto you and believe in the promise you've declared for me. I cast every spirit of Fear and doubts away from my life as I begin to overcome every problem and do great exploits.

Day 9

ALL THINGS COME FROM GOD

"A man can receive nothing unless it has been given to him from heaven." -John 3:27

Man is nothing but a vessel of God. He is a tool in the hands of the Almighty. God is the giver of everything beautiful. Sometimes in life, people make it seem like they are in charge, and that it is through their might they acquired what they have in life. Forgetting that with just a snap of the finger, everything can change.

Often, we make the mistake of relying on a man for help. We keep running to fellow humans for help, instead of going to the Lord. We rely so much on humans and put all our trust and hope in them instead of in the hands of the almighty God. We are quick to forget that it is only God who can touch the heart of man and compel him to do anything.

So dear friend, we are nothing without God. We cannot get anything except it is from him. You can only have a thing when God had said you will. But if God has not spoken on that, you may never have that which you seek no matter what you do. In as much as you have to put efforts towards getting your wants, you have to put God first in that for everything comes from him. If God has not spoken concerning any situation then nothing about it can change. If God does not give you, you might not have it. If he does not permit it, then it will never happen. Let us learn to always go to God for everything we need. He is the sole provider.

PRAYER POINT:

Father, make me realize that nothing can come except through you. Give me the grace to always trust you in everything. Amen.

Day 10

YOU ARE ONE WITH GOD

"Everyone who is called by my Name, whom I have created for My glory; I have formed him, yes, I have made him." -Isaiah 43:7

Imagine how disjointed our families will be if we all decide to bear our names instead of our father's name? Our names bind us together because it is our identity. You are not likely going to enjoy the privileges attached to a name if you are not associated with that name. Part of the privileges attached to associating yourself with God's name is His glory. God's word for you today is centered on being glorious, but the requirement is to be called by His name.

Do you know what it means to be created for the glory of God? It goes deeper than living as a constant reminder of God's supremacy and prowess. The glory of God encompasses; grace, favor success, breakthrough, blessings, mercy, comfort, and the likes. This is not something to be placed out of; this is something to be involved with.

Whose name comes to your mind at every slightest life disarray? To whom do you always run to whenever the burdens become so unbearable for you to shoulder alone? The name you carry in your heart is traceable to where you run to whenever the enemies strike your door with arrows to set you on your toes.

You've got to let God be the center of your life; let Him be whom you see in all you do. Your life has to show that indeed, you are God's own, the apple of His eyes. Only then can the glory He has created you for will have a meaning to the world because you won't be an empty vessel, but a vessel unto honor.

Every man is formed from the dust of the earth, but other breeds of the human race are not just formed but are also made to carry God's weight of glory. God wants you among these new breeds of a chosen generation whose identity is first God. He has a commitment towards them as their Father and blesses them with glory.

You should join these new brands of people by carrying a unique identity in God. Your story is about to change for good. The whole narrative is about to be changed in your favor. God's eternal weight of glory will start shining in you and through you for all to see as you embrace God's identity.

PRAYER POINT:
Oh Lord, I love and identify with your name, I desire from now on to continually make you my number one, and I receive by faith the benefits attached to bearing your name.

$\mathcal{D}$ay *11*

GOD'S ULTIMATE PLAN
FOR YOUR LIFE

"And we know that all things work together for good to those who love God, to those who are called according to his purpose."- Romans 8:28

Assuredly, nothing happens to you without God's consent. God knows about the things you are going through right now, and He has everything planned out perfectly for your good.

Truthfully, God does no evil, and in Him is no wickedness of any sort. He made everything good and beautiful, including you. Then, why do you think He wants to bring hurt, pain, sorrow, and sadness to your life?

You see, the devil is cunny and the originator of all evil. He knows that God has an ultimate plan to give you hope and a beautiful future. But, the devil knows he cannot undo what God had already done. Therefore, he comes up with different gimmicks, deception, distraction, and challenges to make you lose hope and become faithless in the Almighty God.

For instance, God came in the likeness of a man in the person of Jesus, to redeem humanity to Himself. However, the devil thought it in His craftiness to bring Jesus down through the crucifixion death of Christ on the cross. But the Bible says:

"We speak the wisdom of God in a mystery, the hidden wisdom which God ordained before the ages for our glory, which none of the rulers of this age knew; for had they known, they would not have crucified the Lord of glory."-Corinthians 2:7-8

Glory to God! You see that. What the enemy meant for evil was part of God's plan to bring salvation to you and me.

Likewise, the devil cannot stop you from getting to your destination. He might throw pebbles on your path to your destination, but will never be able to stop you because; those stones you see on your path are stepping stones to your greatness. Know this assuredly that God has your best interest at heart.

PRAYER POINT:
Father, I choose to rest in the assurance that you have set all things to work for my good, help my faith, dear God.

Day 12

HE WHO SINGS PRAISES, PRAYS TWICE

"Therefore by Him let us continually offer the sacrifice of praise to God, that is, the fruit of our lips, giving thanks to His name." -Hebrew 13:15

The wall of Jericho, as described by theologians, is the most massive in the Old Testament. Aside from its exceptional height, its thickness is as wide as a dual-lane modern-day road. It will take about five years of intense laboring to bore a passable hole on this wall using ax and shovel considering the bars of iron, concrete and refined stones used for the wall. The wall made Jericho a secure place for her surrounding inhabitant. It will only take the kind of miracle God did over the Red Sea to pull down the Jericho wall. But rather than doing such a miracle, God instructed the Israelites to walk around the city each day while they blow the trumpet of worship before the ark of God. And that shout of praise should be added on the seventh day while they walk around the city seven times. What their ax and shovel could not do in five years, their praise and adoration did it in just seven days.

31

It is difficult to praise God amid intense heat, but these methods have proven to be the fastest. Paul and Silas were praising God in prison and their chains fell off miraculously. Jesus would thank God as a prelude to raising Lazarus from the dead.

Singing God's praises alone is a breakthrough. The enemy does not want to hear you sing; all they want to see you do is complain, worry, and abuse God. Doing the opposite of what they expect irrespective of what you go through is a strong step in anticipation of your new dawn. Praise God today consciously. Dance and sweat if you can, there is so much power in your praise. It will pull down your obstructions, raise you from your dead state, remove your shackles, and push you higher in the spirit.

In this phase of life, the more you show appreciation is, the more you receive. You don't even have to wait to obtain before you show appreciation and gratitude. When you wake up in the morning, God should be whom you reference in your life, and just for the reason that your loved ones are hale and healthy is enough reason to tell God that He is right in your life.

What you have and have not achieved should not determine your attitude to give praise to God; your lips should continually carry His praises.

PRAYER POINT:
Thank you, God, thank you, Jesus, I have nothing to offer but to say thank you, Lord. I will forever bear your praises in my mouth, body, spirit, soul, and mind.

Day 13

ALL THINGS WILL WORK IN MY FAVOUR

"And we know that in all things God works for the good of those who love him, who have been called according to his purpose." -Romans 8:28

Do not be anxious about anything. Rather, be thankful because God will cause all things to work for your favor. You see, sometimes you may think God has abandoned you but in truth, He is always by your side. "Be strong and courageous. Do not be afraid or terrified because of them, for the LORD your God goes with you; he will never leave you nor forsake you (Deuteronomy 31:6). Every situation you are in is God's working to bring you into purpose.

God has a way of making all things right in his time and season. Don't feel depressed or overwhelmed by that challenge or problem. Note that for as long as you are a member of God's body, all without any exemption will work together for your good.

Do you remember the story of Joseph, of how he was thrown inside the pit and later sold into slavery by his brothers? He was imprisoned for a false accusation. He was forgotten by a fellow prisoner he helped interpret a dream. All those events look like evil occurrences but at last, it was revealed that all happened in Joseph's favor. If he was not hated and sold by his brothers how would he have gotten to Egypt? And if Potiphar's wife didn't lie against him he would have served and died as a slave.

In the same way, all that you may be passing through now are God's plans to lift you so high. Can you now see that God is always working in your favor? Praise God!

PRAYER POINT:
Lord please uphold me with your hand and make all things work out in my favor in Jesus's name.

$\mathcal{D}ay\ 14$

GOD WILL COMPLETE HIS WORK IN YOUR LIFE

"...Being confident of this very thing, that He who has begun a good work in you will complete it until the day of Jesus Christ." -Philippians 1:6

How you do think God operates? Do you feel He does things randomly without proper plans? Well, that cannot be true of a God who knows the end of a thing before it begins.

God is a master planner and no situation ever caught Him unaware. There is nothing about you that is strange to God because He knows you even before you were formed in your mother's womb (Jeremiah 1:5). God has well defined your purpose, and he well documented the script of your life. Therefore, whatever happening now in your life will never catch God unaware.

At creation, the bible said that God made Heaven and earth; wasn't that enough for creation? Nevertheless, God knew in His mind what He planned for creation, so He won't stop until He sees that everything He planned looks good, just exactly as He had planned it (Genesis 1:1-31).

Dear friend, you are going through a process of perfection, your current situation notwithstanding. You are a finished product in the sight of God, and He will stop at nothing to making sure you come out perfect, refined, and exactly just the way He had wanted you to be. This is not yet the best moment. This is not your best 'SELF.' God is working on you, and He will not stop till you look like Him.

God will not stop halfway in helping you because it is the God of perfection and completion, and so he will perfect everything that concerns you. Think deeply and you will discover that God has always been faithful. Look at your past, and you will know that things are getting better for you. Can you remember how and where you started? Can you now see where you are today? It is God doing marvelous things in your life.

It will interest you to know that the best of you is yet to come and the greatest things in your life are still in the making. You may think things are not yet the way you want them to be. But, the truth is, things are not the way they used to be. Your best days are not behind you. They are ahead of you, and it means you cannot stop where you are right now. Therefore, do not end God's process of making you while the process is still on.

PRAYER POINT:
God, please give me the confidence to trust in you till you complete your good work which you have started in my life in Jesus name.

$\mathcal{D}ay\ 15$

THE LORD UPHOLD YOU WITH HIS HAND

The LORD makes firm the steps of the one who delights in him; though he may stumble, he will not fall, for the LORD upholds him with his hand.
-Psalm 37:23-24

Consider a child who just began to learn how to walk. The child would stand and fall several times and will be supported while learning how to take a step one after another. However, will the child stop walking because he or she couldn't walk well? Of course not.

Similarly, God wants to walk you through life, supporting you all the way. The storm of life is too boisterous for you to think you can walk through all by yourself. You cannot fight the battle of life alone. You need God. The devil, who is the enemy of God's work, is always at it to destroy humanity. Imagine yourself fighting an age-long being on your own?

The hands of the Lord are stretched upon all nations, and anyone who opens their hands up to take the Lord's hand receives divine help from above. God is willing and always ready to help, support, and carry you through life if you allow Him. You have to let go and allow God.

There are things you have held tightly for too long, and it had limited you in one way or the other. For instance, there are relationships you should let go of because they keep you away from God. The things that have held on to could be what had held you bound. You need to release what is in your hands to allow God to put something new in your hands and walk by your side as you journey through life.

PRAYER POINT:
O Lord my God, helps me to delight in you so you can establish my steps and make me stand firm in you forever.

Day 16

DIVINE ASSURANCE

I shall not die, but live, and declare the works of the Lord.   Psalms 118:17

There is a confidence that comes with worshiping God, an assurance that accompanies believing in His powers and the courage that follows, knowing He will always fight for you.

A believer saying that he shall not die does not mean he won't leave this world. As God has made it, every man must die, but it must be at the appointed time. "I shall not die" means that I shall not die in the hands of men or the hands of my enemies. You may fall sick and maybe close to death's door, but you must be confident that you will survive. A righteous man may fall seven times; he will rise again. You might have made wrong decisions causing you losses of any kind, but you must always stand firm knowing that God can give you double for all your losses. You must be convinced that everything you pass through in life is to the glory of the Almighty God. You can't just die not because it's a boldface declaration but because you have God besides you and that He has promised that thousands shall fall by your side and ten thousand by your right hand.

God promises that you will not be chased hurriedly out of the land of the living. Amid hunger, pains, disasters, plagues, the real children of God shall not die. They shall be favored and shall live to keep declaring God's faithfulness. So while God keeps you alive, worship Him in faith and truth, proclaim on the mountains high, that He is the Lord of Hosts!

PRAYER POINT:
Dear Lord, thank you for saving me from my enemies. May my lips never get tired of praising your name. Amen.

Day 17

HE WILL FIGHT FOR YOU

"For the Lord your God is he who goes with you to fight for you against your enemies, to give you the victor." -Deuteronomy 20:4

Life is like a battlefield, and it takes only the greatest fighters to win the battle of life. No matter how much you train to combat on the battlefield of life, you cannot win the battle on your own because your enemy is not just a powerful destroyer but a strong force in the world that content with humanity daily.

The devil and his agent are always at war with you, making sure you live in frustration, pain, regret, and fulfillment for the rest of your life. He attacks your mind with negative thoughts and brings a situation that is unpleasant to your way. However, the devil cannot win the battle of your life because He was defeated a long time ago. The bible says:

"You, little children, are from God and have overcome them because greater is He who is in you than he who is in the world." -1 John 4:4

Interestingly, you have overcome it already. Never allow the devil to make it appear to you like you are still fighting. You have been given the victory even before the battle started. Walk-in this assurance that God had conquered the devil on your behalf. The battle is not yours but is of God, and you are on God's side. Therefore, quit the victim mentality and begin to see yourself as a winner always because you have a God who gives you the victory for a war He had chosen to fight for you.

PRAYER POINT:
Thank you, Jesus, for the victory I have in God. I take hold of my victory tally in the name of Jesus.

$\mathcal{D}ay$ *18*

HIS GRACE IS SUFFICIENT

But he said to me, "My grace is sufficient for you, for my power is made perfect in weakness." Therefore I will boast all the more gladly of my weaknesses, so that the power of Christ may rest upon me. -2 Corinthians 12:10

Human wisdom and understanding are not sufficient, as it may fail in any situation of life. Your qualifications, social strata, economic resources, and your nation can disappoint you in your time of greatest need. Even your strength may fail you. Despite these, God's grace never fails.

God's grace is His unmerited favor which He gives to all abundantly without measure. God gives His grace as a gift and not a wage you work for or a salary you earn. One of God's demonstration of Grace to humanity is salvation through the sacrifice of Jesus. No human deserves it, but out of love, God gave His only begotten son to redeem humankind to Himself. If God could give Jesus to humanity, He will freely give to you everything you request of Him.

You might have tried in your strength to get what you want. Maybe you have struggled without a result, and you are on the verge of giving up. May I introduce to you the Grace of God, which brings to you result without a struggle? Always remember, God's grace is sufficient in your time of greatest need. The grace of God provides you with the divine ability to change your situation and live a purposeful life.

God's grace makes a weak person strong and restores hope in hopeless situations. It was the grace that saved Daniel from the hands of hungry lions in the den (Daniel 6:22-28). It was God's grace that brought her favor before the king (Esther 2:17). The same grace is available for you today, to save you, transform your life, and bring you into the full promises of God for your life.

PRAYER POINT:

Please, Lord, let your grace never cease from my life. And give me strength in my areas of weakness.

Day 19

GOD ALWAYS GOT YOUR BACK

"No temptation has overtaken you that is not common to man. God is faithful, and he will not let you be tempted beyond your ability, but with the temptation, he will also provide the way of escape, that you may be able to endure it." *-1 Corinthians 10:13*

God does not promise a challenge-free life. What He does promise is that your challenges will not overcome you. He said that when you walk through the shadow of death, He will be with you. No difficulty has the power to overthrow you because God is with you to uphold you. He is in you to comfort you and beside you to walk you through all life's journey of life.

The truth about life is that challenges are inevitable. We grow through challenges and develop strength in the process. You might not appreciate life enough without a reason to strive for something higher and better. Without problems, there will never be a solution. The unexpected will happen. But, whenever all these happen, do not panic. Always remember that God is a specialist in problem-solving, an ultimate

fighter in the battle of life, and a strength for you in your time of greatest weakness.
Jesus said:

"These things I have spoken to you, that in me you may have peace. In the world, you will have tribulation; but be of good cheer, I have overcome the world." -John 16:33

Awesome! Your stability in God is certain, even amidst the toughest situation of life. In God, there is peace, regardless of how turbulent the situation is. Remember that it was God who commanded Moses to lead the children of Israel out of Egypt. Yet, they encountered problems in their ways. At a time, they got hooked in between the red sea and Pharaoh's chariots, and it seemed that was the end, but God came to their rescue; He divided the red sea and made them walked on dry land.

Even Jesus Christ Himself experienced tough times: He was tempted by Satan, encountered a storm in the mid of the sea, and was crucified by enemies. But, in each scenario, God provided the way of escape. He overcame temptation, calmed the sea, and rose from death. That same God is still at work in our time today because He does not change.

So what should you do in difficult times? Trust on God and believe that He got your back and He will deliver you from all the troubles of life. Assuredly, tough times never last; they are not forever. Therefore, do not conclude yourself in your temporary situation. Call on God, and He will surely deliver you.

PRAYER POINT:
O Lord, I receive the power to remain firm in God even in times of trouble because I know that my victory is sure in Jesus's name.

Day 20

I LOVE THEM THAT LOVE ME

I love those who love me, and those who seek
me diligently will find me. Riches and honor
are with me, Enduring riches and righteousness.
-Proverbs 8:17-18

Since you cannot love that which you do not know, to love God, you must know Him. Those who love God know of him, they have seen his loveliness, and they have encountered his goodness and mercy. They must have had encounters where He saved them. They communicate and commune with Him daily. Their love for Him is sincere because it comes from the depths of their hearts. Like metal is drawn to a magnet, they are drawn to Him. They put Him first before everyone and everything. They hold Him in the highest esteem. They listen to His commandments. They follow His words and will always deny themselves and their flesh in order not to offend God.

He made us in His image. He loved us first before we loved Him. He died on the cross to save us from our sins. Making little sacrifices for our beloved ones proves difficult for us, we talk more about dying for them. What love could be greater than this that someone gave His life so that his friends may live? None! God protects those He loves. He undertakes their cause. He blesses them. He consoles them when they cry. He carries their burden and lifts their spirits when they are down. He gives them his grace always. He comes to their rescue when they are in danger. He promises them eternal life in the world after.

God has also promised riches and righteousness to all who seek him diligently. Those who come to Him for forgiveness, for pardon, for grace, for life, and help. All you have to do is to come to Him. His graces are sufficient.

PRAYER POINT:
Father, because you loved me first, I love you with all my heart. Through your loving help, may I live a life that is pleasing to you? Amen.

HE SHALL BLESS YOU OUT OF ZION

The Lord bless you out of Zion, And may you see the good of Jerusalem All the days of your life.
-Psalms 128:5

A man who fears God shall receive spiritual blessings. Every righteous man is a part that makes up God's inheritance. When God sends his blessings on his people, each gets his own. God's blessings go to each household; none is left out.

The question is, why Zion? Zion is described as the city of the Lord, the mountain of His holiness, according to psalms 48:1. It is also described as the perfection of beauty from where God shines (Psalm 50:2). God dwells in Zion to bless His beloved, and that blessing is your divine heritage. The blessing is that you will see the good of the land all the days of your life.

You need to be convinced beyond your present situation that God wants the very best for you in the land of the living. Little wonder every book of the Bible pronounces this blessing over you.   Numbers 6:24-26 says, "The Lord bless you and keep you; The Lord make His face shine upon you, and be gracious to you; The Lord lift His countenance upon you, And give you peace." These are the words of God and His blessings upon the man who trusts in him. You also need to start being deliberate by searching out these blessings out and be assured of each, using them to address every situation you found yourself.

Are you aware that the blessing of God is not limited to only your productive years when you have the strength to do many things? His blessing is for each day of your life. No matter your age, you are covered with this blessing. This should get you so excited. Hallelujah!!! All the days of my life are full of blessings...

PRAYER POINT:

Father, I believe I am covered with the divine heritage of spiritual blessings from heavenly places in Christ. All the days of my life are blessed because I serve the God that rules from Zion.

Day 22

ALL THINGS ARE POSSIBLE

"And He said to them, "Because of the littleness of your faith; for truly I say to you, if you have faith the size of a mustard seed, you will say to this mountain, 'Move from here to there, and it will move, and nothing will be impossible to you." -Matthew 17:20

According to human standards, there are certain things considered possible and others impossible. Impossibility is the limitation of the human race. Your ability is limited to certain things you can handle. Imagine if you have the power to do anything you wish to do in your life. Awesome! You will be surprised to know that truly you have such power, but you have not been exercising it.

God is limitless. Nothing is impossible with Him (Luke 1:37). However, He has put inside you the power to do anything, including the impossible. You were created in the image of God and His very own likeness. Interestingly, the Bible declared that "You are gods, and all of you are children of the Most High" (Psalm 82:6, Romans 8:11).

51

The same power that makes creation possible resides in you. God had given you an authority to declare whatever you want, and nothing shall be impossible with you. However, only those who know this right exploit it. The Apostle of faith called Paul said:

"I can do all things through him who strengthens me. "
-Philippians 4:13

Awesome! Your authority is in Christ and not in anything else. There is no impossibility with you because you are identified with God through Jesus Christ. It will interest you to know Jesus Christ is the word of God through whom God spoke the world into reality. Subsequently, the same word of God has power on your lip, but you need to speak it upon any impossible situation to see the result you desire.

PRAYER POINT:
I declare because of the word of God that nothing shall be called impossible in my life from now henceforth.

Day 23

THE SECRETS HE HAS REVEALED ARE OURS

The secret things belong to the Lord our God, but those things which are revealed belong to us and our children forever, that we may do all the words of this law. -Deuteronomy 29:29

There are many things about nature which are kept a secret, away from a man but known by God. There are many secrets about God himself, which we humans do not know or comprehend. Notwithstanding that he reveals himself to us, there is a lot about this infinite being which remains beyond our comprehension, as the three divine people in one God, how God thinks before he takes a decision, the merge of two natures; human and divine in Jesus Christ, what is the faith of children who died at infancy, when one will die, what time and in what way will we die, amongst others.

However, there are many other things that God has revealed to us including his laws and commandments which we should obey with all our hearts, his promises which are for us and our children, and the duties of religion.

The ones which are revealed to us are for our use and practice. We are to put it into action for what will be the essence of the revelation if we do not practice the words of God. The scripture encourages us not just to be hearers but also doers of the word of God.

While many things about God and providence remain a mystery, some things that we are sure of our God's mercy, his faithfulness, his goodness, and, most importantly, his love. He loves us to the extent of laying down his life that we may live. Let this fact never leave our minds. May we always be encouraged to love God more, to listen to him, to follow his words. Call upon Him whenever we need him, and he always answers.

PRAYER POINT:
Father, May I always follow your words and obey all your commandments for you are the King forever and ever. Amen.

Day 24

GOD SAID IT SHOULD BE SO

For He performs what is appointed for me, and many such things are with Him. *-Job 23:14*

Despite Job's condition, He believed that God will perform what he has been appointed for him and that there are many more still to come. He refused to curse God and die like he was advised. He never for once stopped believing that God approved his trials. So he was willing to go through them, whatever comes his way. He did not know the plan of God, so he vowed not to question him. He realized that it would be in vain to resist whatever God says will surely come to pass.

Often, life gives us one of its bitter pills. We swallow it with a glass of complaints and doubts. The truth remains that as children of God and believers of the word. Nothing can happen in our lives without the father being aware. Sometimes God approves those temptations because he is planning something greater for us. Other times, he wants to strengthen our faith. He may not be angry with us, but such sufferings may be part of his eternal plan.

So when we face crises, trials, tribulations, and suffering, let us not see it as something which is happening but as chance. We should instead see it as part of God's plan. It will help us accept our pains calmly and bring our minds to rest for the father's promise to grant us the grace to sustain whatever trials he sends us. Though we may not at that moment understand God's reason, it will help us accept our sufferings as part of God's plan. Remember His words that He will never allow temptations that are greater than us to come to us.

Whenever you find yourself in a bad situation, understand that there is a divine purpose for which that is happening. You might be surprised that whatever you passed through may be part of God's higher plan, which extends to all things. Whatever you are passing through, know that you are not alone; there may be others in such situations that are looking part of God's plan. Since we cannot know his thoughts except the things revealed to us, let us stand strong in our faith and never doubt the love of God. You should also pray about any situation you find yourself in but never doubt God, for he has a reason for everything.

PRAYER POINT:
Father in my difficult moments, may I never doubt you. I will console myself that everything happening to me is approved by you alone. Amen.

Day 25

TRUST HIM WITH ALL YOUR HEART

Trust in the Lord with all your heart, and lean not on your own understanding; in all your ways acknowledge Him, And He shall direct your paths. Do not be wise in your own eyes; Fear the Lord and depart from evil. -Proverbs 3:5-7

The verses above are hinged on three things; trusting God, acknowledging, and fearing Him. The first verse urges us to wholly rely upon God's power, wisdom, and goodness. We should also depend on him for directions and help in the course of life. The second limb of that verse tells us not to rely on our human understanding to accomplish our desires. This is to say that without God's blessings, we cannot achieve anything. Our human strength and knowledge are not enough. Thus, it is unreliable. We should also not put our confidence in our friends, families, and relatives; they may disappoint too.

The second verse tells us to acknowledge the Almighty God in all that we do. We can't, if we don't keep following His directions, counsels, trusting in his wisdom, goodness, and power, and performing all our duties in a way that glorifies His mighty name.

A man cannot Judge his case in court, so it's not in your power to say that you are wise. We are encouraged to fear the Lord and avoid all evil and wrongdoings.

It is only by obeying the Lord's commandments that we will enjoy peace and happiness. Though we may not live long on earth, obedience to him leads to everlasting life. God's mercy is real, and his faithfulness is without end. Let us learn to trust God with all our hearts knowing that he will do what is best for us always. We should take comfort in him. Those who trust in humans or their power fails. Always strive to do that which is lawful. Let us also acknowledge God in all that we do. We must acknowledge him with thanksgiving and submission to his words. Ask for God's grace, always to live a better life.

PRAYER POINT:
Lord Jesus, direct my path so that I may walk in the way of light and truth. May your words guide me all the days of my life. Amen.

Day 26

HE OPENS TO YOU HIS GOOD TREASURE

The Lord will open to you His good treasure, the heavens, to give the rain to your land in its season, and to bless all the work of your hand. You shall lend to many nations, but you shall not borrow.
-Deuteronomy 28:12

God's treasures are for us. We are his people, and he loves us. Rain is one of the treasures of God; without it, man will go hungry. It is the rain that makes our crops grow and gives us food. We get enough water to drink because of the rain which God sends to the earth.

God said he would open the heavens and pour forth rain on all the earth so that the works if our hands shall be blessed. Work of your hands may in the world of today mean different things. The world has changed, and occupations are no more limited to farming and cultivation of the land. We have lawyers, teachers, engineers, traders, sewists, nurses, doctors, event planners, and a host of other diverse works.

Does it mean then that the blessings of God are only raining, to favor only the farmers? Not at all. God's blessings are not limited to one form or a set of people. The rain in the above verse is a metaphor to represent the blessings of God.

The Almighty has promised to bless whatever you do. However, your handwork must be an honest one. God does not bless people who do the things frowned at by a man and himself. You cannot be a thief and expect God to bless you, for his 5th Commandment states that you should not steal. For God to bless your handwork also, you must carry out your business in a transparent manner.

God has promised to bless you richly that you may lack nothing. You will be a lender but never a borrower. If you are having any crises in your workplace or business, call on God, pray to him, and tell him about your challenges. He will come to your rescue because he has promised to bless the work of your hands.

PRAYER POINT:
Father, thank you for all your blessings and mercy. I pray that you continue to shower me with your blessings. Give me a good heart to help others whom I'm better than. Amen.

Day 27

HE WILL TURN YOUR SORROW TO JOY

"For his anger is but for a moment, and his favor is for a lifetime. Weeping may tarry for the night, but joy comes with the morning." -Psalm 30:5

God does not find delight in seeing His handiwork suffer. You are God's favorite handiwork and it is part of His plan for you is that you always be happy. God himself is joy and that is why there is always fullness of joy in His presence.

Sorrow, pain, anguish, and every form of evil entered the world ever since Satan had been sent here. Satan is the author of sorrow and sadness. Satan is the number one enemy of mankind. He doesn't want anyone to live in peace and enjoy God's fullness of joy. But God is always there to favor you and to give you joy.

God is still in the business of turning mourning into dancing. If he did it for Jabez, Hannah, Esther, Abraham,

Ruth, and others in the scriptures; be rest assured that your problem is not too big for him; He will do it for you too.

The Bible says in John 16:22 that, so also you have sorrow now, but I will see you again, and your hearts will rejoice, and no one will take your joy from you. No matter what you may be passing through now, it is just but for a moment. Remember that tough times never last but tough people do. God is your strength. He will turn all your sorrow to joy according to His unfailing promises.

God's word assures you that though weeping may endure for a night, joy comes in the morning (Psalm 30:5). So rejoice, because God will soon turn your sorrow to joy!

PRAYER POINT:
O Lord my God, let my joy come now according to your word.

Day 28

HEAVEN IS MY SOURCE

"John answered and said, "A man can receive nothing unless it has been given to him from Heaven." *-John 3:27*

What have you tried to do? How long have you wandered about looking for rest from all the challenges life throws at you? Consider the stress you went through before you got that little comfort and how long it took before it evaporated again. You often time find yourself at the same point you began with not long after you enjoyed a little rest from different battles here and there. Yes, you won't say there are no solutions to your problems at all; they just don't last before the problem resurfaces again with more complexity. Maybe because the source of the solution determines for how long it works.

No one will buy the product of a company that has been flagged by quality assurance agencies. However, a good product can be ascertained from a good manufacturer. If your methodology of escape is man orchestrated, you can be sure that the same man can negate his good deeds at the slightest provocation from external forces. If your solution is sensual or logically propelled, it will only be but for a while.

Here is the good news: God wants to bless you with the real blessing that comes from above. The kind that cannot be compared to what human effort, logic or nature can give. The kind of blessing that no eyes have seen before, that no ears have heard. He is only waiting for you to lookup.

The allocation is made ready for you. You only have to lift your eyes to heaven from where your help comes (psalm 121:1). Know it assuredly that any wisdom that does not descend from heaven is earthly, sensual, and demonic (James 3:16). Our God is from above, and He is above all things. Let him give you those good things He had prepared for you since the foundation of the world.

No matter how good or attractive earthly blessings may appear to you, it is nothing as compared to what God desires to give you right now. All you need to do is to sign up with faith in your heart, and the rest will be testimonies. This God is ready to save, are you ready to be saved?

PRAYER POINT:

Dear God, help me to look up to you for each of my needs. I only want what you will give, help me to always live with the consciousness that it is only your gifts that are eternal and are without variableness.

Day 29

GOD CARES FOR YOU

*"Casting all your care upon Him,
for He cares for you" -1 Peter 5:7*

When you tell people going through hard times that God cares, they wonder if he truly cares. How could you tell someone who just lost a contract that God cares? How would you show a person who had been bedridden for months that God cares? How would you tell a nation whose community had just been stricken by the worst disaster that God cares? How would you even say to a community of impoverished and dying children that God cares?

Surely, in these entire situations, it will be hard for anyone to believe that God truly cares for them. But do you think God does evil? Truthfully, there is no evil with God at all because he is all good, caring, and loving God, and he seeks to show forth his goodness to humanity always. Your present situation can never nullify the goodness of God. Please, never believe the lie of the devil in your situation for the devil is the author of all evil (John 10:10).

However, whatever you have lost to the devil, God is set to give you a double portion of it as a replacement. Your loss is not your end. Do not think that God does not care about your loss. He allows it so that you can get the better offer He has in stock for you. What you lost was not God's best yet because eyes have not yet seen what God had prepared for you. Surely, there is more for you than this!

God is interested in our prosperity more than you feel so concerned. He desires the best for you more than your quest. God wants to see to it that you are happy with life more than you wish. However, He wants you to take your eyes off the situation and focus on Him alone. The bible says:

"Looking unto Jesus, the author, and finisher of our faith." -Hebrews 12:2

Shift your focus from the bitterness of the situation to the joy of having God as your father. Regardless of what the case might look or feels, know that you have a God who is more concerned about you, and He is ready to see you through all life trials and temptations.

PRAYER POINT

Lord Jesus, I choose to focus my attention on you rather than dwell on my pains. I choose you over every of my life challenges, hurts, pains, and regret. Thank you because I know you care for me.

Day 30

THE PRESENCE OF THE LORD

***"The mountains melt like wax at the presence of the LORD, at the presence of the Lord of the whole earth."* -Psalm 97:5**

No obstacle, difficulty, and impossibility dare to stand against God's presence. The presence of the Lord brings joy, happiness, fulfillment, and freedom forever. Your life becomes fruitful and graceful when the Lord is with you. People struggle most times in their daily endeavors because they have never allowed God. With God's presence, you will have the grace to run effortlessly, the strength to go beyond and above, the power to challenge opposition without fear, and the boldness to stand against all the odds.

Life is full of challenges, many of which you cannot solve on your own without a divine assistant. There are troubles of life that had caused you so much struggle, and you seem to lose yourself in the process of solving these problems on your own. But I have good news for you today. God said:

"And He [God] said, My Presence will go with you, and I will give you rest."-Exodus 33:14

Perhaps you have been struggling, and it seems like a vicious cycle of repeated failure. Maybe the mountain of impossibility keeps staring at you on the face, and it looks like there is no way out. All this while, you have been trying on your own to sort out things, but it had always hit a dead end. Why not allow God today? The truth of the matter is that your wisdom and power can fail you at some points in life, but the wisdom and power of God will never fail.

You need the presence of the Lord henceforth. Let your day begin with Him and end with Him. Until you have submitted your whole life, thoughts, ways, means, plans, dreams, strategies, knowledge, and person to Him as LORD overall, you cannot carry His presence. This kind of presence is the one that only comes with the LORD. Jesus is God's gift to man, and that is all you need in your life. When Jesus is in your life's boat, the storm of life ceases, impossibility give way, sorrow melt away, and your struggle becomes over.

Let Jesus be the Lord of ALL in your life. He wants to take over everything that concerns you. Therefore, I want you to submit everything at the feet of Jesus today. Jesus is Lord over all the earth, and this is your victory.

PRAYER POINT:
Lord Jesus, I agree I have faced these mountains and hills all by myself, and I have failed. Now, I submit all Lordship to you in all things; take over Jesus and challenge all my mountains. I withdraw for you to show up and melt all mountains right away. Thank you, Father, for in Jesus's name I have prayed.

Day 31

GOD IS GREATER THAN ALL YOUR PROBLEMS

"You, dear children, are from God and have overcome them, because the one who is in you is greater than the one who is in the world." -1 John 4:4

God is omnipotent. He is the only God who can do all things. He created all things! All power in heaven and on earth belongs to Him. So, you don't need to be afraid of anything. Whenever you are confronted by any difficult situation, just "Look to the LORD and his strength; seek his face always (1 Chronicles 16:11). Call His attention to your problem and He will act on your behalf because He is able to do all things.

Indeed God is great and mighty. His superiority and greatness cannot be overemphasized. The scriptures say, *"Now unto him, that is able to do exceeding abundantly above all that we ask or think, according to the power that worketh in us. Unto him be glory in the church by Christ Jesus throughout all ages, world without end. Amen." (Ephesians 3:19-20).*

God is God all by himself, he doesn't need an extra inch to be better or greater. He is God, the great and mighty one. Hence, the gigantic nature of your problem, the fatness, and robustness of that which challenges you, cannot be compared to His mightiness.

Nothing can withstand the mightiness of God, not even your problem. Choose to always look unto God in times of challenges and not your situation.

PRAYER POINT:

From today, I receive the grace to live with the full assurance that greater is He that is in me than the he that is in the world.

Day 32

MY HELP COMES FROM GOD

I will lift my eyes to the hills—from whence comes my help? My help comes from the Lord, Who made heaven and earth.   *-Psalms 121:1-2*

We always look to the strong for strength. Those who live in the valley are prey to many illnesses and disorders to which there is no cure. So they sometimes resort to the mountains for safety.

A hill is a small mountain. Like a mountain, a hill is strong and reliable and could be a temporal escape route. It's a pseudo help that is capable of making you miss the real thing. David looked to the hills and resolved to make God the source of his help. God is the only reliable being; even the hills cannot be trusted. Help only come from above, looking elsewhere is in vain.

What does this hill represent? A man faced with many challenges can resolve to go to church. But if you ask him sincerely, he might believe so much in the pastor of the church than in God. That's why the church building is filled with a lot of persons who don't know God or believe in him. Their intention may be to get connected with a prominent person in or to get a contract or any other reasons different God. The church can be a hill, and sometimes, the hills can proffer a specific solution.

 In a bid to distract you, the devil will thrust so hard to veil your face from seeing your faithful helper. David said, my help comes from the Lord, not from the hills. You have to fight and refuse to be blindfolded by the devil by not giving him a chance to supply pseudo help that won't last the test of time. We should look up to God's promises, his mercies, his divine goodness, and providence. The Lord grants safety to all who trust in him. He never allows anyone who runs to him for safety to come to any harm. He is calling you to come. He is extending His arms of grace to you. All you need is to look up to Him, communicate with Him through prayer, and your sorrows shall become a thing long forgotten.

PRAYER POINT:
Lord, all of my help comes from you. Help me to see you clearer than never before as my only Helper. Amen.

Day 33

GOD LOVES YOU

"For God so loved the world, that he gave his only begotten Son, that whosoever believeth in him should not perish, but have everlasting life"
-John 3:16

It is true if you take time to ponder on how well you have lived; despite the trying and difficult times, despite the weird and awful times; you will be able to recognize and see adequately that God loves you.

Living life with an understanding that God loves you is essential for purposeful living. The more we walk in the light of His love, the clearer life becomes to us.

God has shown through diverse means and methods that you fill His heart. He has done all to prove His love to us. One thing the devil tries to do a lot of times is to make us feel we aren't loved. The devil tends to put us in a position where we are separated from God.

However, in Romans 8:35-39, the bible says,

"Who shall separate us from the love of Christ? shall tribulation, or distress, or persecution, or famine, or nakedness, or peril, or sword? As it is written, For thy sake, we are killed all the day long; we are accounted as sheep for the slaughter. Nay, in all these things we are more than conquerors through him that loved us. I am persuaded, that neither death, nor life, nor angels, nor principalities, nor powers, nor things present, nor things to come. Nor height, nor depth, nor any other creature, shall be able to separate us from the love of God, which is in Christ Jesus our Lord.".

It is an impossible case for us to be separated from God's love. Though God hates sin, he loves sinners and through Jesus Christ our Lord, He has made a means of eternal atonement for all our sins.

His eternal will is that you abide in his love. He cherishes everything about you and delights in your fellowship. He loves you and wants you to love him in return.
 It's true fellowship and love cannot be disjointed, since obedience and love cannot be separated. If you love God, you will make fellowship paramount. If you love God you will obey His commandments (John 14:15)

PRAYER POINT:

Thank you Father for loving me. Daily as I live and often as I breathe, Lord Jesus please help to respond appropriately to your love.

Day 34

UNDERSTAND YOUR TIMES AND SEASONS

"To everything there is a season, a time for every purpose under heaven:" -Ecclesiastes 3:1

The Lord will not do anything on the earth without attaching a time to it. Likewise, every of God's work in your life has its times and seasons. Time is the instant of an event while the season is a period of an event. A season is the summation of times that defines the period over which an event takes place. For example, the time of pregnancy is different from the period of pregnancy. The time of pregnancy is the instant of conception in the woman while the period of pregnancy is the time from conception to delivery. What do these things mean and how do they apply to you?

Understanding your time will let you know the instant a thing begins or ends in your life. It is the moment a change takes place in your journey, whether towards the positive or the negative. You must be able to keep track of what takes place in your life and when it takes place to know who is at work in your experiences. Just as God works with times and seasons in the earth, so also the devil works with times and seasons in the earth. Don't live your days without tracking the movements in your life. There is a time that God begins to do a thing in your life; you must know it. When He ends that same thing, you must know it. The period an experience will last in your life is a season. No challenge is there before you without the duration allotted to it. If you will keep your head up and your eyes on God, the season will end and a new thing will begin.

Nevertheless, whatever the devils do in your life must not be allowed to complete its season. This is because, in the end, you might have lost major virtues in your life. Whenever you discover an activity of the power of darkness around you, don't let it survive. If the devil puts vanity in your labor, and you don't check it out early, you might waste 10 years of your life struggling and laboring without any fruit to show for it. Keep track of the moves of Satan concerning you. Let no seed sown in your soul and body see the light of the day. Bring all things under God's authority in prayers and destroy the works of darkness. You will surely be helped by God.

PRAYER POINT:

Heavenly Father, God of all times and seasons, have mercy on me and let all evil seasons end in my life and begin a new season for me today. In Jesus's name, I have prayed. Amen.

Day 35

YOU ARE NOT ALONE

"No temptation has overtaken you except such as is common to man; but God is faithful, who will not allow you to be tempted beyond what you are able, but with the temptation will also make the way of escape, that you may be able to bear it."- *1 Corinthians 10:13*

You are one of many believers going through the tough times of life. You have a company of tested and tried ones. You are never alone. What you have gone through has been experienced by someone somewhere in the world and the same God who delivered them is alive to deliver you.

The Bible is full of stories that are peculiar to us today, though in diverse ways. They were not alone, and you are not alone. You have the company of others, passing through similar things you are going through now and they are also trusting God for help. Don't you think God will help you? What about Daniel? What about Esther? God didn't allow them to perish in their perils and you won't perish in yours.

The God of times and seasons will move the hand of time
for your sake and things will change for you. Don't be
deceived by the way people aggravate a man's situation by
pitying him or sympathizing with him, you are not alone and
you have the help of God at hand. God is so close to you
now more than He was even with Joseph. Do you believe
this?

PRAYER POINT:

*Dear Lord Jesus, I know now that you will help me as you
have men of old and my fellow believers the world over. I
again put my trust in you and in your integrity to see me
through in this world. Thank you for helping me. In Jesus's
name, I have prayed.*

Day 36

COMFORT OTHERS

"Who comforts us in all our tribulation that we may be able to comfort those who are in any trouble, with the comfort with which we ourselves are comforted by God." -2Corin. 1:4

God expects you to comfort someone today, just as he has comforted you. The previous lesson explained to you that you are not alone in what you are going through now. Some people went through the same things in their generations and were comforted by God. Now you are being comforted by their comforts. You have read in the Bible how God had delivered Joseph, Daniel, Esther, Meshach, Shadrach and Abednego, Jeremiah, Paul, and other men and women who went through sufferings and were delivered. You also have heard of men and women today who at some time in their lives, have had to face death and yet were delivered by God. They speak of their comforts in the Word of God and you too are being comforted.

Likewise, you must seek to comfort others that are going through similar storms that the LORD is bringing your way. Don't overlook the pains and troubles of others. Having known how much you help you received from God in such a situation, offer to help them as well. Help to fix a business. Help to heal a wound in a soul. Help to lift a burden. Give as much as you have received. It is wickedness to watch on while others go through all the troubles you went through without offering them a helping hand. You might say, 'they have to go through theirs; I went through mine. This is not godly.

Your friend doesn't have to spend five years in depression because you spent five years in depression. Snap him or her out of the grip of the spirit of depression and do that quickly. You might have spent quite a several years in poverty before you finally made it. You don't have to let your sibling go through the same struggles before you could help. With that comfort, you received from God, comfort others, and help them. Joseph had suffered loneliness, hunger, pain, hurt, and dejection yet he went about relieving everyone he met of their pains and frustration. He would not watch others fall into the ditch he fell into or leave them in the ditch if at all they fell into one. Comfort others with the same comfort you have received from the Lord today.

PRAYER POINT:
God of patience and comfort, I thank you for comforting me in my entire situation as it is today. I ask that you forgive in any way I have left others to their pains and I have overlooked others' sufferings. I commit to helping others see you in all their challenges. So help me God. Amen.

Day 37

COME TO ZION (PART ONE)

"They go from strength to strength; each one appears before God in Zion." -Psalms 84:7

Zion is a place on a mount in Jerusalem where God chose for Himself in the old covenant, to dwell in and to meet with His people. God placed His mark on Mount Zion and set it as a mount of deliverance. If anyone suddenly found himself in Zion, though he was bound, he would be delivered. It was the city God chose for Himself to reveal His presence and impart grace and strength to all who appear in Zion. It was upon Mount Zion that the Temple Solomon built stood and from there the name of the God of Abraham, Isaac, and Jacob was proclaimed throughout the surrounding nations. What was it about Zion that made nations go to her? It was the Presence of LORD God.

Today, Zion is no longer us a geographical place in Israel; it is a spiritual place where we stand before God. Zion is a spiritual city full of the redeemed of the Lord Jesus; those who have been washed clean by the Blood of the Lamb and have had their names written in the BOOK OF LIFE. If you are part of Christ Jesus, then you have an inheritance in this city of God. Every believer has a place in Zion and all believers are expected to know this truth. Your inheritance is in Zion

.

Amongst other things, your strength is in Zion. Come to Zion! Leave the futility of men's help and appear in Zion. For they go from strength to strength that appears before God in Zion. No one appears before God in weakness and weariness and look up to God for help and is rejected. It is God's faithfulness to fill you with new strength and anoint you with fresh oil when you appear before Him in Zion.

Zion is where the LORD is. It is the City of the Living God, where all men are made alive from the dead. It is the company of fellow resurrected believers. It is the fellowship of faithful men and women. It is where you meet with men of like passions and pursuits. It is where you see the big picture over and over again. It is the place where the smoke vanishes and only sacrifices are offered unto God. It is the place of renewing. Have you found Zion where you are? Do you know how to get there? Do you go there always?

PRAYER POINT:

They that appear before God in Zion shall go from strength to strength. Lord, I come to Zion today and I appear you. I ask that you have mercy on me and give me strength for the journey ahead in Jesus's name. Amen.

$\mathcal{D}$ay 38

COME TO ZION (PART TWO)

"They go from strength to strength [increasing in victorious power]; each of them appears before God in Zion" -Psalm 84:7(AMP)

There are two dimensions of Zion: the material and the immaterial dimensions. The tangible Zion is the physical assembly of Believers who have been resurrected which could be called the Church. Just as a nation is both a place and a people so also Zion is a place and a people. The two dimensions must be incorporated to partake of the inheritances of the saints in Zion. The material Zion is the coming together of faithful beings in Christ who have come to worship God and to seek His face. This could be a local assembly, a campus fellowship, or even a group of young ones meeting to pray. It is a physical unit of Zion and it has in itself the share of the inheritances of the men and women who meet to worship. Are you a part of a company that worships the Living God? Have you found a physical unit of Zion, where you are that you can be part of to have your share in the inheritances? That is where your strength is.

You may have decided to stand alone and fight alone, but you are not covered. There is no much strength in aloneness. Always, two are better than one. How much more three or four or ten or even a hundred? Zion is not designed for one man. A tree is not called a forest. A king is not a kingdom. You cannot be alone and expect to possess your possessions in the world. You must be part of a unit in Zion and there become a fellow-partaker of the inheritance of the saints in the light. Will you find your unit in Zion and be part of it?

PRAYER POINT:
Great God in Zion, I have seen how weak and vulnerable I would be if I exclude myself from the people in Zion. Please help me find my place in Zion and let me obtain my inheritance therein in Jesus's Name. Amen.

COME TO ZION (PART THREE)

"But you have come to Mount Zion and to the city of the Living God, the heavenly Jerusalem, to an innumerable company of angels, to the general assembly and church of the firstborn who are registered in heaven, to God the Judge of all, to the spirits of Just men made perfect, to Jesus the mediator of the new covenant, and to the blood of sprinkling, that speaks better things than that of Abel." -Hebrews 12:22-24

The other dimension of Zion is the immaterial dimension. The company of spirit beings that are in charge of the material dimension and are superior to the material dimension. This is the real Zion where the source of strength is. Every physical unit of Zion is designed and meant to take men to the spiritual Zion to appear before God. Every local assembly of believers is meant to transport men to that place where they stand before God. Every fellowship is designed to lead men to fellowship with spirits that dwell in Zion.

If you are part of an assembly and you are never led to appear before God; you have not reached Zion. If you meet with people to pray and you do not know the presence of God and Christ, you have not found Zion. If you have not encountered the Blood of Jesus Christ and you are not being washed from your filthiness, you have not found Zion. When you find Zion, you will find out that you are never alone. You will always have a company of mixed spirits—the angels and the believers. You cannot be in Zion and remain in depression. You cannot come to Zion and not know why you are living. Confusion and frustration leave in Zion. What a wonderful place to be! The blind eyes are opened. The weak arms are strengthened. The deaf ears are opened, and life becomes new again. It is a meeting of immortals and immortal things happen.

Have you truly found Zion where you are? If yes, then come to Zion straight away. Don't stand alone and waste away. There is strength for you in Zion. Thousands of spirits of just men are waiting for you. You enter into the mighty assembly of believers (both material and immaterial) in the living God, and you cannot be stranded anymore. Hallelujah!

PRAYER POINT:
Halleluyah!!! I go to Zion to meet my God in Jesus's name. Whatever that has kept me away from the company of believers I break it away in Jesus's name. Amen.

Day 40

COME TO ZION (PART FOUR)

***"They go from strength to strength; Each one appears before God in Zion."* -Psalms 84:7**

Another thing to consider in Zion is that only those who appear before God will go from strength to strength. Not just all who come to Zion. It is not everyone who comes to Zion will be strengthened but only those who appear before God. Some have only come to appear before men. They only end up being part of the physical unit of Zion.

They are not known in the general assembly of the saints in heaven. They don't transport with others in worship to stand before God and to obtain strength. They have only come to appear before men and to show that they are around. Their minds are not about the heavenly Jerusalem but all about the things that are seen and touched. This group of believers will never know God for themselves neither will they be strengthened by God. They will continue to hear of what happened to many others who indeed appear before God, but they will never know it for themselves. After a while, they will be envious of others who have received strength from their meeting with the Living God and not just with men. They may even go further to withdraw themselves from the physical unit of Zion in which their inheritances are. Whose fault is this?

You may also fall into such error if you are not conscious of what you do when you appear in Zion. You come to Zion to appear before God and not before men. Not before friends and relatives. You have to appear on Mount Zion, to stand before your LORD God.

PRAYER POINT:

Lord Jesus, in your name, I ask the Father to show me the pathway to appear before Him as I fellowship with other believers. Amen.

Day 41

HIDE NOT YOURSELF

"Woe to those who seek deep to hide their counsel far from the LORD, and their works are in the dark; they say, 'Who sees us?' and 'who knows us'"
-Isaiah 29:15

The final thing you must see about this appearance is that it is not unto condemnation but unto strengthening. You can hide before God in Zion. While the Scripture urges that we appear boldly before God in Zion, many still tend to hide their ways from God. This kind of people will never receive strength. They will go back to depression. Strength doesn't come to those who pretend to be something they are not. Strength only comes to the honest and sincere. Those who agree that they are weak and in need of God's strength will have it.

You will not know God's help if you seek in your heart to play hypocrisy. If you want to appear in Zion to show fellow believers how much strength you have when you inwardly weak and wasted, then you will never receive the strength of

God that only comes to the honest and open. In Isaiah 40:28-31 says:

"Have you not known? Have you not heard? The everlasting God, the LORD, the Creator of the ends of the earth, neither fails nor is weary. His understanding is unsearchable. He gives power to the weak, and to those who have no might He increases strength...but they that wait upon the LORD shall renew their strength..."

Pretense before God will get you nothing but more and lasting weakness. Come to God in full sincerity and Honesty, whatever state you are. He is both merciful and compassionate to cleanse you from all unrighteousness and forgive you all sins and after that, give you all the strength you need to live victoriously.

PRAYER POINT:

My Father in heaven, I open up all my deep thoughts to you, and I decide to acknowledge you in all my ways and to tend to hide before you. I know you see all that I do and that I cannot truly hide anything from you. Please help me now in Jesus's name. Amen.

Day 42

GOD IS ABLE

Now to Him who is able to do exceedingly abundantly above all that we ask or think, according to the power that works in us.
-Ephesians 3:20

No one is as powerful as God. God's power is large and extensive. It reaches the edges of the earth and above. God does things that are impossible before men. He can do all things except things that contradict his nature, inconsistent with his purposes and decrees, and any other thing which to do would be to deny himself.

Our father can do more than we ask. He knows our needs, he understands us. Before we ask, he had already made provisions to solve our needs. We also need God's spirit to know how to ask and how to ask right. Sometimes we grumble that God did not answer our prayers when we do not ask right. In requesting favors from God we have to ask in faith believing that he will do it. Also, we have to be consistent and have the spirit of perseverance. Often we are not consistent in our prayers, we request for something from

God today, the next time we will remember to ask God again will be after many weeks.

At times, God may not do what we asked of him because he has something greater in store for us. It could also be that giving us that which we ask at that moment could make us fall out of faith.

The spirit of God in us is enough evidence of God's exceeding powers. He will continue to work with us, providing us with whatever we need. His work of grace will continue in us till the end. Let us never lose our trust in God for he is able.

PRAYER POINT:
Father, I testify that all powers in heaven and earth belong to you. Thank you for all the good things you have given us. Amen.

Day 43

YOUR KINGDOM COME

"Your Kingdom come. Your will be done on earth as it is in heaven." -Matthew 6:10

The kingdom of God describes the area of influence of God in a place. To what extent does a society comply with the will of God tells the level of the reign of His kingdom in that society. A kingdom talks of a community of people who are in agreement to live together and to be ruled by one man. It would not be a kingdom if there were no people to reign over. It will neither be a kingdom if there were no king to rule over the people. A kingdom is only complete when there are a king and a people to reign over. A kingdom can be established with two: one to rule and the other to be ruled; one to be served and the other to serve.

Likewise, the coming of the kingdom of God is about the coming of a people (or a person) and the coming of their (or his) king. It is not just about the king or just about the people but about the king and his people. "Your Kingdom Come!"

can be said to mean "your people come with their king." If you reject a king, you have rejected his people. If you reject a people, you have also rejected their king. What do these things mean to you?

As a believer, you are both a kingdom and part of a larger kingdom. The larger kingdom is the whole church of Christ in heaven and on earth. But as an individual, you are a kingdom in yourself, in partnership with Jesus Christ, the king in your heart. Therefore, whenever you cry, 'your kingdom come!' you are saying, 'Jesus come, and I come'. You are saying, 'Jesus reign in me!' Jesus must reign in you before he can reign in the world. Jesus must reign in each believer for him to reign in our society or the government. If he is not reigning in you by His Holy Spirit, He cannot reign through you anywhere. If you are not serving him as a believer, no one can serve Him because of your life. Have you unreservedly submitted your whole life to the rule and lordship of Jesus? If not, then you must begin to pray that His kingdom comes in your life.

PRAYER POINT:
Let your reign be established in my heart that I may not rule. You reign in me, Jesus. Amen.

Day 44

TRUST GOD NOT MAN

I said in my haste, "All men are liars.
-Psalms 116:11

David was a king with many loyal allies that are true and faithful to him. II Sam 23 is a chapter in the Bible dedicated to highlighting how faithful the mighty men of David were and how some of them endangered their lives to serve David. There were three among his men that fought through the camp of the Philistine to draw water for David from the well Bethlehem just by hearing David's wish to drink from the well of Bethlehem. Despite having trusted chiefs, faithful priests, loyal armies, and good subjects that will lay their lives to serve him, David still concluded that all men are liars. Though this he said in haste, yet it could only mean that good deeds can be done in lies.

All men are liars has become a common phrase in today's world. Men disappoint if you put your trust in them. But the word "haste" in the verse of the Psalm shows that the Psalmist was quick to conclude. He was prompt in making decisions and may not have appropriately analyzed his statement before publishing it.

However, are all men indeed, liars? Paul, in Rom 3:4, said, "let God be true, and every man is liars." In other words, we can say that let God be true, and all flesh be lairs. Man is so frail and cannot be trusted for anything irrespective of how good he is. God, on the other hand, is not a man that will lie nor the son of man that will repent of His word. Man can change his words, his good deeds, his hand of favor, or help at the slightest provocation, pressure, or trouble. This is why you cannot invest your trust in men irrespective.

Of course, you may have men who are trustworthy, reliable, and truthful. Friends whom you can verge for and people who have always been there for you. The fact that they have disappointed you one time or the other is a sign that they can't be depended on. God's word for you today is that cursed is the man that trusts in man, and makes flesh his arm, and whose heart departs from the LORD (Jer 17:5). Put all of your faith in God; there is neither variableness nor shadow of turning in Him

PRAYER POINT:
Father, give me the grace to always put my trust in you and not to depend on a man for every one of my needs. Amen.

Day 45

GOD'S WILL FOR THE EARTH

"Your Kingdom come. Your will be done on earth as it is in heaven." -Matthew 6:10

The Message Bible renders that same scripture as 'set the world right; Do what's best—as above, so below.' The King James Version renders it this way: 'thy kingdom come. Thy will be done in earth, as it is in heaven.'

These renditions reveal that there is a will of God for the earth that can only be established or performed when His kingdom comes. The earth must be ruled as heaven is ruled and the inhabitants of the earth must be like the inhabitants of heaven—in submission to the will of God and of His Christ. Just as a believer cries out that the will of God be done in him and on him, the earth also cries out for the will of God to be done in it and on it.

But what is the will of God for the earth? Amongst others, the will of God for the earth is liberty; Freedom from the bondage that came through the fall of man. And this will

97

only be established as the kingdom comes. As you have understood, that the coming of the kingdom is both the coming of a king and his people; it will follow that the freedom of the earth lies on the shoulders of a people and their king.

Are you a child of God? Then the earth's liberty rests on your shoulders, together with other children of God. If all you live for is yourself and all that concerns you, then you are not doing the whole counsel of God for you. You are a son of God to establish liberty for the captives of the mighty and to set free the oppressed. You have been liberated to liberate others. Will you rise to your responsibility?

PRAYER POINT:
Lord Jesus, the great Deliverer, I thank you for delivering me from the power of darkness. I, this day, ask that you open my eyes to see the captivity of the world around and to attend to it by your grace and power. Amen.

# Day 46

THE ROD OF HIS INHERITANCE (PART ONE)

"The portion of Jacob is not like them: for he is the former of all things; and Israel is the rod of His inheritance: the LORD of hosts is his name."
-Jeremiah 10:16 (KJV)

Just as we say the LORD is our portion, the LORD also says we are His portion on earth. In all the families of the earth, the LORD God has chosen His people as His inheritance. This was revealed in the way God took the physical nation of Israel, in the old covenant, as His inheritance. That is if you were to ask God personally to tell you what He owned on earth; He would say, 'Israel.' He said it clearly in Amos 3:2 (MSG), that 'out of all the families of the earth, I picked you…' this means that both in the old covenant and in the new covenant, God chose people for Himself.

Why does God choose a people for Himself? It is to send them out as a rod of His inheritance. This is a sense of Possession God has concerning anyone that is called by His name. God has chosen you to own you. God has called you to be part of His family to be the LORD over you and to expand His inheritance in the earth. You may say that God owns all the heavens and the earth, which is true; and that all souls are His. You are right.

However, possession is different from an inheritance. An inheritance is what you get as a share of an entire property. By Creation, God owns all. But by Redemption, He does not own all—He only has a share in all. The whole world belongs to God because of creation, but by Redemption, only a few belong to Him, and that is His inheritance in the earth.

If you are part of the Kingdom of God, then you are in His inheritance. And he has a plan for you. He has something to do with you. He has a working plan for your living on earth, and He surely has an expectation. He expects you to live with the consciousness that you belong to Him without any rivalry. He wants to see that no one else shares you with Him. You are His inheritance—your body, your mind, your spirit—everything! When the when natures divided the whole world, you fell into His side by redemption, and you are one of many that have become His own both by the creation and by redemption—completely His own. Have you realized how much you will hurt Him to live your life as if you don't belong to Him?

PRAYER POINT:
Father, what a wonderful thing it is to know that I am part of your inheritance on the earth! I repent of my ways without your Lordship, and I commit myself to follow you as the absolute owner of my life. Thank you, Father; in Jesus's name.

Day 47

THE ROD OF HIS INHERITANCE (PART TWO)

"The portion of Jacob is not like them: for he is the former of all things; and Israel is the rod of His inheritance: the LORD of hosts is his name."
-Jeremiah 10:16

A rod is generally known to be a straight, round stick, metal, or other material. But in the mind of God, as revealed in the pages of the Bible, a rod is a person or a people that is useful by God to establish His rule on the earth. And there are several times in the past that God has revealed to us in types and forms, the rods of His inheritance. To understand these forms and the mind of God in them, you will need to follow through several passages that are taught subsequently.

Now, what does God do with the rod of His inheritance? God does these following things with the rod of His inheritance:

- He drops the rod
- He sends the rod
- He stretches the rod
- He strikes with the rod

However, the first rod of God that appeared on earth was Adam, and he was dropped by God in Eden to do His will (see Genesis 2:15). He was the first form of the rod of His inheritance dropped to establish His government in the earth. But he lost it, and God had to find another way to establish His government on earth.

Before you continue, you must understand that God must form every rod of God before it can be useful to God and usable by God. Before Adam was placed in Eden, He was formed. He was cultured and treated. You cannot be lawless and at the same time, be useful to God. You cannot escape God's process of forming you into what He can use, and you still expect Him to use you in the kingdom. He must form you into His desired shape and fashion before He can do much with you.

PRAYER POINT:
Lord, form me into what you can do much with me this kingdom.

Day 48

GOD DROPS THE ROD
(PART ONE)

"So the LORD said to him, 'what is that in your hand?'
he said, 'a rod.' And He said, 'cast it on the ground.'
So he cast it on the ground, and it became a serpent,
and Moses fled from it." -Exodus 4:2-3

A typical example in the Scriptures, where God revealed His mind in dropping the rod of His inheritance, is that of Moses. And from this, you will see the mysteries in the rod of His inheritance.

First, you must remember that the rod in the hand of Moses was previously used to lead and strike the flock of sheep owned by Jethro, the Midianite. It was an ordinary rod. Nothing was special about it before this encounter with God. But as soon as Moses encountered God in the wilderness, everything changed about the rod and what was ordinary became extraordinary and Moses himself had to run away from his rod. This means that you may be ordinary

103

before, but as soon as you encounter God in His power, you become extraordinary, and it will not matter what you used to be. All that will matter is that you have met the LORD and you have been changed.

Secondly, the idea of dropping the rod was not Moses' idea but God's idea and God's command. The rod must have dropped many times while Moses led the sheep in the pastures, without becoming anything strange. He had dropped it many times whenever he returned home, yet nothing happened. But when God commanded him to drop it, it turned to a serpent. Until God has spoken to you, nothing can be extraordinary about you. You may copy what others do and dare to say what others say, yet it will not amount to anything if God has not spoken to you.

PRAYER POINT:
O Lord my God, speak to my life that I may walk in the extraordinary.

Day 49

GOD DROPS THE ROD
(PART TWO)

"When Pharaoh speaks to you, saying, 'show a miracle for yourselves,' then you shall say to Aaron, 'Take your rod and cast it before Pharaoh, and let it become a serpent'" -Exodus 7:9

This verse of the scripture reveals why God has told Moses to drop the rod in the wilderness; God wanted him to do the same in Egypt before Pharaoh and his wise men. God knew Moses would encounter opposition and would be required to show them a miracle. So God began with Moses in the wilderness.

Whatever God will do with you before men, He will begin with you alone in secret. If God makes you a minister to nations, He will begin to work on you in the secret as you minister to Him in worship. If He ever sends you out to challenge the kings and princes of the world and to bring them under the rule of His kingdom, he will begin the work in you while you meet Him in your secret place. What He will do through you in public is only an extension of what He is doing with you in secret.

Furthermore, God has determined to make you a miracle. You are the one He wants to show when the world requires Him to show them one. That rod in Moses' hand was God's answer to the demand of Pharaoh. Wait on God; you are a miracle in the process. The same way He has made many other believers a miracle in their generations He will make you one in your generation if you wait on Him enough in prayers and worship.

Have you given up your commitment to the secret meeting with the LORD? Have you canceled yourself out of the people enlisted for a miracle? Yes, you are still His concern; the rod of His inheritance, and He will drop you as a miracle when He has wrought His ways in you. Wait!

PRAYER POINT:
O Lord, do your work in me that I may become the miracle the world is waiting.

Day 50

GOD DROPS THE ROD
(PART THREE)

"So Moses and Aaron went in to Pharaoh, and they did so, just as the LORD commanded. And Aaron cast down his rod before Pharaoh and before his servants, and it became a serpent. But Pharaoh also called the wise men and the sorcerers; so the magicians of Egypt, they also did in like manner with their enchantments." -Exodus 7:10-11

Today, you will see that the enemy has many counterfeit miracles to show you also. The devil wants you to distrust in public what God has told you in secret. He wants you to doubt what God has done in you while you were in secret. He will put up every smoke to confuse you when you show up. But God has an answer to it.

God never told Moses that the wise men of Egypt could and would also do the same thing God asked him to do. But they did it. However, the difference was clear. The rod of God would always swallow up the rods of Satan.

You must know, that just as God has rods in His hand to establish His kingdom on earth, the devil also has his rods—his share of the entire property—which he uses to establish his kingdom in the earth. But whenever the rod of Satan encounters the rod of God, he is in trouble, and an end comes to him. Whenever a son of the devil meets with a son of God, he gets into trouble, and he regrets ever meeting the son of God.

You are not to be confused or afraid when you see the things the devil is doing around you, wait on God and do what He has said to you; eventually, you will prevail over all the works of darkness. The strongest weapon in the hand of the devil is fear. If Moses had fled again when the wise men dropped their rods, most likely their rods would have prevailed. But thank God, he was not afraid. Don't be afraid; you are stronger than the rods of darkness. The one who has spoken to you and sent you will not leave you to become prey to the devil. He will surely see to it that you prevail over the sons and daughters of darkness, for you are light.

PRAYER POINT:
I declare today that every confusion and fear the devil has put in me to make me doubt God and His Word vanishes right now in Jesus's name. Amen.

Day 51

GOD DROPS THE ROD
(PART FOUR)

"So the LORD said to him, 'what is that in your hand?'
he said, 'a rod.' And He said, 'cast it on the ground.'"
- Exodus 4:2-3

Finally, before we go on to other things that God does with the rod, we will consider the dropping of the rod itself. God said to Moses, 'cast it to the ground.' We will break this into its part and what it means to be dropped by God.

The statement 'Cast it to the ground' reveals two things: how it should be dropped and where it should be dropped. To place something on the ground is different from casting it to the ground. Casting means throwing it to the ground. It is not likely done gently. It could even make a sound. It is like when you don't want a thing anymore, and you want to let it go. It is so with you, although God still wants you. When you are about to be revealed by God to the world as a miraculous rod in his hand, you will go through tough times. You may not even feel like anything supernatural is present in you. You feel rejected and cast away and cast down. It's like the heavens are closed and your prayers have been wasted. You may even have thought you were born to suffer because this is a moment when God has just cast you to the ground.

However, His casting you to the ground is for a purpose. You were cast down to be lifted higher. Look at what is about to happen to you in the spirit and give God the glory. God cannot forsake you though it appears like that. You are right in the heart of God. And you will see what a miracle He is making of you.

The second thing is where He chooses to cast you. He said to Moses, 'cast it to the ground.' Not to the sea or into the air, but to the ground. It is the LORD who determines where you must be to become that miracle. You don't choose a place for yourself in the kingdom; He chooses your place and your role and invariably your inheritance in the kingdom. Wherever God has chosen for you, no matter how difficult it is now for you, stay there.

PRAYER POINT:
Lord Jesus, I know today that you have a place for me where you want me to be. I pray that you lead me to the very place I will fulfill your purpose for me in this kingdom.

Day 52

EXCEPTIONAL FAVOR

"The Lord is near to all who call upon Him, to all who call upon Him in truth. He will fulfil the desire of those who fear Him; He also will hear their cry and save them."   -Psalms 145: 18-19

Whoever seeks the face of God shall see His face in all their endeavors. You can't expect that should God answer to you when you do not call on Him, nor stay truthful to Him in all your ways. The Spirit of God works in truth. He dwells in a heart that bears truth and righteousness.

Now, God has promised to stay near to those who call upon Him, and not just call upon Him but those who call upon Him in truth. Have you convinced yourself that God can save and protect you? If not, how do you expect to receive from Him?

Look, you can deceive yourself but not God, He sees through your heart, the thoughts of your mind, and your undone action. So, you should start being truthful to yourself and God as you call upon Him. Men often use God as a cover-up or as their second option if their logically planned moves should fail. Calling God in trust means you completely put all your trust in Him. It's either God or God, no other option.

God has promised to always hearken to you when you cry unto Him in truth, pouring all the burdens that make your heart heavy on Him. What it takes from you is to communicate with Him in a true heart. Take the doubts away from your heart, lean on Him completely, and watch if God is capable of changing everything or not.

God has promised to save you, so what are you still waiting for? What are you holding unto? Don't let false things take you away from the true promise of God. There is assurance in God and in everything that He does or says, which is why we have to make sure we stay near to Him every time of our lives. There is no fear of evil when God is in our lives, neither are there doubts that he doesn't abide with us.

PRAYER POINT:
God, give me the heart of truth that when I call upon you, you will hear my cries and save me. Put in me the fear of God and grant all my desires.

Day 53

NEW THINGS

"The name of the Lord is a strong tower;
the righteous run to it and are safe."
-Proverbs 18:10

Praise the name of the Lord, your strong tower and fortress. Hallelujah to God who has provided shelter, shield, and protection in His holy name. His name does not just protect us by strength; His name also protects us by height. A tower is high beyond reach, so those whose habitation is in the name of the Lord does not only stay preserved but are also out of reach from every oppressor of life. No matter the number of the crowd pursuing an armed bandit, once he crosses or enters a police station, everyone withdraws except on invitation maybe to get their statement. If an armed bandit has a safe place from death, how much you are a son of God.

It is about time you start to call upon that name of the Lord; it is not time for you to slack on calling His name, it not a time for you to give up, neither is it time for you to seek refuge outside the name of the Lord.

Run as fast as you can into the tower of the Lord, let Him take over every one of your worries, let Him be the one to shield you. Is there anything that can be done without God's protection in your life? Nothing catches God by surprise because He has everything all figured out, all you need to do is sit back and watch how God covers your life with His supreme protection. Don't hope on any man, no protection can supersede God's.

Reference the name of the Lord and His promises; let it have a hold in your life. Get rid of whatever it is that would stop you from calling upon His name. The name of the Lord is very powerful; even demons tremble at the call of that name, the name of Jesus, the name of God.

PRAYER POINT:
God, keep me in thy sight safe that I may dwell in your strong tower all the days of my life because I know you will never fail me.

Day 54

HAVE YOU PRAYED?

"And when He had come into the house, his disciples asked Him privately, "Why could we not cast it out?" So He said to them, "This kind can come out by nothing but prayer and fasting."-Mark 9: 28-29

As a believer of God, doing the impossibilities goes beyond knowing the norms or process. If you wouldn't like to break the norms, the beyond norms will not come. The disciples were still basking on the norms, whereas things have gone beyond the norms. What are those things you are still doing as norms? Friends let's do beyond the norms which require PRAYER majorly! Have you been attempting to get something done, you are qualified but you never get hold of it? Pray about it. Have you been experiencing a downfall? Pray about it? For those things that look either good or bad, pray about it. It's time to pray. Your kneels are requesting for activeness, your place of prayer is ready. Pray and keep praying until it becomes a reality. This kind can come by nothing but by prayer....

PRAYER POINT:

Father, I receive the grace to pray, for everything I have lost in times past, I recover all through your mercy. I choose to pray always.

Day 55

THE FAITH THAT PRODUCES RESULT

"If you have faith and do not doubt, you will not only do what was done to the fig tree, but also if you say to this mountain, 'Be removed and be cast into the sea,' it will be done." -Matthew 21:21

The Bible in Hebrews 11:1 defined faith to be the substance of things hoped for, and the evidence of things not seen. Interestingly, Abraham was called the father of faith for his utmost trust in God. He showed unwavering faith when God promised him a son even after he and his wife had passed the age of children bearing. And when he was asked to sacrifice his only son Isaac, he did it without question.

Do you remember Noah? Noah had faith and trusted God. God assured Noah that he will save him and his family in the flood that was to strike the earth and Noah believed God with all his heart. He followed God's instruction intently to build an ark and ensured that all that believed him were in this ark.

You see, it is hard to find this kind of unwavering faith in our age and time. Many believers are alien to God's instructions and directions. They do lip service to God and only believe him when things seem to go well with them. In the face of challenges, their faith weaves. They shake, doubt, and question the power of God.

God's word to you today is simple. Your faith can change everything about your life forever. With faith, you can do a lot of things in the name of Jesus. Faith makes the impossible possible and brings to fulfillment the promises of God. Your faith does not have to be in a particular size for it to effect changes. All you need is just to believe what God says, that settles it all.

PRAYER POINT:

Dear Lord, I know I'm a weak human full of doubts. Feed me your grace that I may believe and never doubt your words again. Amen

Day 56

DOES GOD KNOW YOU?

"I am the good shepherd; and I know my sheep, and I am known by my own. As the Father knows me, even so I know the Father; and I lay down my life for the sheep."
-John 10:14-15

Many people know there is God, but the sad of it is, God does not know many as His children. There's a difference between God knowing you as one of his creations and God knowing you as His Child! Do you know God? Does God know you as His child? When you put so many children in a room, and you have the mothers or fathers in the next room, if one child cries, there's a certainty that the actual mother or father will recognize the voice because they know each other. So likewise, God hears and knows our voices or faces. Who are you to God? How much of God do you know? How close are you to him? You can make Him know you today, is never too late friend.

PRAYER POINT:
*I call you Father, yet I don't know you, Jesus I am ready to
be known by you, I give my life to you in exchange for your
life, I am called your own. Amen.*

Day 57

LET IT GO!

"Then his master, after he had called him, said to him, you wicked servant! I forgave you all that debt because you begged me. Should you not also have had compassion on your fellow servant, just as I pitied you?"
-Matthew 18:3-33

He hurt me! She got me angry! I can never forgive him or her! Are these your words or decisions for that person that got you angry? I understand, and I am fully aware what the fellow did was wrong and you truly deserve to be bitter. I know it's painful and s/he needs to get paid back in his coin. Can I say something? Please let it go! I know it is hard, but please, let it go! You don't want to carry a lot of people in your mind and heart with bitterness, because it will tell on your health physically and spiritually. I say again, let it go!

Who are those that have offended you? List them out or bring out if you have a diary of offenses people did to you that you keep, bring them out and begin to forgive them one after the other. Release the person so that you also can enjoy this beautiful life. When next you see the person that offended you, smile and hug (if you can), you can also have lunch together. The time the devil has lay hold of your joy is over; get it back.

PRAYER POINT:

Father, I release everyone that has hurt me and those I have offended I ask for forgiveness. I let them go freely. I have joy unspeakable. Amen.

Day 58

REJECT CHEAP COMFORT

"Then Elkanah her husband said to her, "Hannah, why do you weep? Why do you not eat? And why is your heart grieved? Am I not better to you than ten sons?"
-1 Samuel 1:8

Some people meant well when seeking to lift the burdens and pain in our lives, but there is continual grief that is a necessary precursor for a personal breakthrough. Cheap comfort seeks to take away your pain and burdens are premature comforts that bring a temporary pleasure; it does not deal with the root of the issues but hinders you from seeking heaven's intervention.

Elkanah tried to present himself as sufficient consolation to Hannah, but she needs more. She knows what she desires. She needed more than Elkanah; she needed a child of destiny that will take away her stigma and reproach.

You need to be like Hannah today, never be comforted by cheap comfort, inform of empty soothing words, gift, or short cut that have the potential of truncating God's divine agenda for your life.

PRAYER POINT:

Lord, may I never seek or accept cheap comfort until you bring all that is in your mind into manifestation in my life. Amen.

HE WILL STRENGTHEN YOU

"Though the fig tree may not blossom, nor fruit be on the vines; Though the labor of the olive may fail, And the fields yield no food; Though the flock may be cut off from the fold, And there be no herd in the stalls."
-Habakkuk 3:17

Some people meant well when seeking to lift the burdens and pain in our lives, but there is continual grief that is a necessary precursor for a personal breakthrough. Cheap comfort seeks to take away your pain and burdens are premature comforts that bring a temporary pleasure; it does not deal with the root of the issues but hinders you from seeking heaven's intervention.

Elkanah tried to present himself as sufficient consolation to Hannah, but she needs more. She knows what she desires. She needed more than Elkanah; she needed a child of destiny that will take away her stigma and reproach.

You need to be like Hannah today, never be comforted by cheap comfort, inform of empty soothing words, gift, or shortcut that have the potential of truncating God's divine agenda for your life.

PRAYER POINT:

Lord, may I never seek or accept cheap comfort until you bring all that is in your mind into manifestation in my life. Amen.

# Day 60

WITHIN YOU A BLESSING IN DISGUISE

"So Elisha said to her, "What shall I do for you? Tell me, what do you have in the house?" And she said, "Your maidservant has nothing in the house but a jar of oil." -2 Kings 4:2

Have you ever wonder what causes when many times we put our hope in people to provide solutions to our immediate needs and yet we couldn't get any help from them? The woman in the text was hopeless and needed help urgently. She cried out to the prophet with the hope he will give her an instant solution to her predicaments, only for her to be asked if she had anything in the house. The prophet pointed to her the solutions to her predicaments are right in her house. Check within; you could have the solution.

Amazing! How it will be when you could solve many things you have expected people to help you. Look within; the solution is right in there. It could be your son or daughter, your husband or wife, your relative or friend or that lost relationship you need to bring back. The blessing is right there; look carefully.

PRAYER POINT:

Father, open my eyes to see the untapped blessings around me. Help me to identify and utilize optimally the available resources you have given me. Amen.

Day 61

GOD IS ALWAYS NEAR

"The Lord is near to all who call upon Him, to all who call upon Him in truth. He will fulfill the desire of those who fear Him; He also will hear their cry and save them." -Psalms 145:18-19

Life is a shade of many colors. Sometimes you get a mix of it like a rainbow, and other times it all goes black or grey. Sometimes life leaves us sad, lost, and confused. There could be times you lose loved ones. Other times life issues could break you and leave you depressed. There are those nights you hug your pillows on empty stomach and cry all night long. There could be times you work hard but still can't afford your needs. There are times you fail to provide for your children and their tears break our hearts.

These are times you feel that God has forsaken you and you ask, why should I obey him? Why should I honor him? Why should I believe his words when he cannot be there in time of my needs?

You see, in our moment of grief, pains, and weakness, we easily doubt God's love. We query his existence. It is human to feel the hurt and experience such pain. Nevertheless, your situation will never make God less or keep a distance from you. God is always near especially in our most devastated state.

Whatever we lose might not be ours initially and if it was ours, then he permitted the loss because he has something better in stock for us. Our challenges or incapability that causes us hurt and pains are not an act of God. God does no evil. Every good is from him. Therefore, when a situation strikes hard, always know that God will never let you down and do any wicked act. He is close to you always, more than the clothes you are wearing.

PRAYER POINT:

Father, give me the grace never to forget you in my moment of weakness. When the going gets tough, hold my hand, and never leave my side.

Day 62

MY IDENTITY

"The Spirit Himself bears witness with our spirit that we are children of God. And if children, then heirs—heirs of God and joint heirs with Christ, if indeed we suffer with Him, that we may also be glorified together."
-Romans 8:16-17

Can I meet you? What is your name? These are some of the questions being asked on the first contact. What to look out for when meeting for the first time or searching for an individual is to get the person's name. Even a face without a name is faceless. When you meet someone for the first time and proper acquaintance, you introduce yourself with your name. Your name is powerful as this captures your identity. Who are you? What do people call you? What do you call yourself?

When you are down, your name is lifted, when you are sick, your name is healthy, when you are broke, your name is wealthy, and when all hope is lost, your name is Christ in me, the hope of Glory! When the devil asks for my identity, I tell him I am a child of God, an heir of God, and a Joint Heir with Christ. I cannot be defeated; I am glorified. This is who I am. Hallelujah!

PRAYER POINTS:

Father, in the name of Jesus, I confess and proclaim that my identity is in Christ, I am no longer called forsaken, I am a Child of God, I am an Heir of God and a Joint Heir with Christ, this is who I am. Amen.

$\mathcal{D}ay\ 63$

A FRIEND INDEED

"Greater love has no one than this than to lay down one's life for his friends. You are my friends if you do whatever I command you."
-John 15:13-14

You can tell a lot about a person by the company they keep. Many at times, the type of friends we keep can do either good or damage to one's personality. There's this saying; "show me your friend, and I will tell you who you are". I tell you that the company of your friends is the major determinant to shape one's life. Who are your friends? Do they add or multiply to you? Or do they subtract and divide your life? To what extent can your friend go for you?

"A man who has friends must himself be friendly, but there is a friend who sticks closer than a brother." -Proverbs 18:24

There's a friend who can go to any length for you. He's someone who can give up all in his possession just for you. There was a time he decided to lay down his life in other to redeem his friends. What a great friend is he? Don't you wish to have that kind of friend?

PRAYER POINT:
Father, I have found in you a great friend, thank you for laying down your life for me, please, Lord, I ask that you keep being my friend. Amen.

Day 64

HOLDING ON

"Whenever I am afraid, I will trust in you."
-Psalm 56:3

Have you ever wonder what assures babies they will not fall whenever they are being thrown up? They most assuredly knew the hands that threw them up would surely catch them when coming down. This is trust. I know you can be going through trials and difficult times; I want you to put your trust in God for he knows about it. His arms are wide enough to catch you; he will never allow you to fail or be defeated. He is always there for you. Hold on; your testimony arrives soonest.

PRAYER POINT:
Father, I will trust you, because I know, and I am assured you never fail. Amen.

Day 65

YOU ARE SHIELDED

"As the mountains surround Jerusalem, so the Lord surrounds His people from this time forth and forever." -Psalm 125:2

Life has a lot of phases. It can be very hectic sometimes, as it comes with its ups and downs. Often, it leaves us drained, tired, and fed up. Some persons who cannot take it may slide into depression, and others contemplate other dangerous things. Today God wants to remind you of how important you are to Him.

You see, your government may fail you, and your most trusted friend could disappoint you. But the Lord said, I will never leave you nor forsake you (Hebrews 13:5). God's promises to us are real and true. Everyone else might desert you but the Lord will never leave you. He is with you always both when all goes fine and even otherwise.

The bible says;

"Trust in the LORD with all your heart, and lean not on your understanding, in all your ways acknowledge Him, And He shall direct your paths."
-Proverbs 3:5-6

We all know that 'trust' is a very sacred thing. The father understands this too. He knows that when you trust Him completely, it means putting your life in his hands. Assuredly, I want to tell you that whatever you put in the hands of God is secured forever.

If God can keep you this far, He can still see you through many years to come. You just have to put all your trust in His mighty hands. Trust God like a baby who is helpless without Him. Trust Him for the air to breathe in. Learn to trust Him such that the very air you breathe in and out is God. However, your proof of trust is revealed in obedience. You go where He wants you to go and do what He wants you to do.

The truth of the matter is that you cannot feel God's presence when you do things anti-God. God is always near those who obey Him and keep His commands, and His shield of protection is around His Children. Do you trust God? Are you His Child? Do you obey Him? Then surely, you are protected and your destiny is preserved forever.

PRAYER POINT:
Lord, I'm sorry for the many days I doubted your Almightiness. Father, I trust you with my life and believe your word that you will never leave me nor forsake me.

Day 66

YOUR MIRROR

"You shall teach them diligently to your children, and shall talk of them when you sit in your house, when you walk by the way, when you lie down and when you rise." - Deuteronomy 6:7

Research has proven that children's first teachers are their parents and the most effective way to learn is to watch what the parents do. The question is; how effective have you being a teacher to your children? Your children are your mirror; they reflect the real you to the outside world. How close are you to your children? Understand their world, system, timing, and season. Win the heart of your children, make them see you as their role model indeed, not in a forceful way but in an acceptable way; teach them the way of the Lord as early as when they started talking. Get them gifts, take them out, and imbibe in them a good culture and character so that they can represent you well even in your absence. Pray for them, correct them in love, encourage them, and praise them when they achieve some feats. Your children are your reflections!

PRAYER POINT:

Father, I thank you for the wonderful gifts you have given me, I commit them into your hands, please keep them, help me to train and build them in your way Lord, let them reflect your glory. Amen.

Day 67

INCREASE YOUR CAPACITY

"Your word I have hidden in my heart that I might not sin against you." -Psalm 119:11

Men in their bid to build chest, muscle, and physical fitness, find themselves constantly going to the gym. Before you say Jack Robbins, the tiny looking man is now built up and can go for a macho competition.

As believers, our gym is Bible study and prayer meetings. Here, we build our spiritual capacity to become a terror to the kingdom of darkness. How often do you go to the gym? Or when last have you done a personal gym at home (personal bible study and a time out to pray)?

Waiting for a free day when you will have long hours may never come if that's your plan, but you can adopt the little by little method. The little method is a feasible time out you create for each day to read the bible and pray. You don't want to wait till you are faced with trials, temptations, or attacks of the enemy before you remember Psalms does not have 151. Start today, read a verse per day or adopt a yearly bible plan but pray every day, be consistent with it, and before you know it, you have grown over time.

PRAYER POINT:

Father in the name of Jesus, I choose to read your word and pray every day, please Lord give me strength and grace. Amen.

Day 68

OPEN ARMS

"But God demonstrates His own love towards us, in that while we were still sinners, Christ died for us." -Romans 5:8

No matter how painful a child may hurt his or her parent, the child will be forgiven, though s/he may serve some punishments for the wrong actions. However, Christ had loved us and died for us even when we were still wallowing in sin. He is so thoughtful of us that He chooses to open wide His arms to us till we all come back to repentance. He doesn't mind how far or deep you have gone, how dirty you are; all he just wanted is that you come back home to his embrace.

Today is the gift you have, don't attempt to procrastinate it may not do you good. Right there where you are, be sincere with yourself, open up your heart to Him and confess your sins and wrongdoings to him, ask for mercy and forgiveness, then ask him to be your savior and Lord of your life.

Hallelujah, welcome to the family of God. Going forward be assured that he had embraced you and you are hidden under his shadow going forward.

PRAYER POINT:

Father, in the name of Jesus, thank you for saving me, and please help me Lord not to return to my old life. Amen.

Day 69

THE RIGHTEOUS SHALL NOT STUMBLE

But the path of the just is like the shining Sun, that shines ever brighter unto the perfect day.
-Proverbs 4:18

As Christians called to be followers of Jesus, our lives should be a true example for others. A beacon for others to follow. As sons and daughters of God, we are the light of the world. Therefore we illuminate both our path and that of those walking with us. Non-believers should be able to see us and ask, "Whom do you imitate? I want to be like you?"

On the other hand, in verse 19 of the chapter above, we learn that the path of the wicked is like deep darkness, they do not know what makes them stumble. Having God comes with an added advantage, light! With God on our side, our paths will be full of light and we shall for no reason stumble or fall. Every day, we encounter situations that make us think we are failures to ourselves. We feel like we are walking down a narrow dark path.

That is not so, these trials and tribulations are but a test of our righteousness. It is what we have to pass through as children of light. Of course, the devil will keep on trying but all his plans shall fail. So ask yourself today, are you truly the light to others whom you are called to be? Have others truly learned from you how to live better lives? As believers, let us work hard and amend our ways so that others may learn positive things from us. May we be a shining light to others that they may find the light through us.

PRAYER POINT:

Lord, give me the grace to be righteous. May I be a light unto my generation and may my path continue to be a shining sun. Amen.

Day 70

HE OFFERS PEACE

"The Lord blesses you and keeps you; The Lord makes His face shine upon you, and be gracious to you; The Lord lift up His countenance upon you, and give you peace." -Numbers 6:24-26

Peace is not all about your life is perfect; it's about showing himself as God in every storm of life. It is peaceful when God is in it. Many people confuse quietness with peace. A person can be in a quiet environment yet his or her mind is at war with difficult issues of life. However, in peace, no matter what happens around you, nothing else moves you except the fact that you have God for you.

Dear friend, God has promised you peace and He will back it up with an assurance of hope and a great future. Your tomorrow is secured in God. So, stop the feeling of doubt and the fear of what if it does not work? If God could have you in His plan, then, He is more than able to bring you into the fullness of this plan. Quit worrying and start believing.

The storm will rage. The fire will burn. Challenges will come. But you must always remember that in all, you have the prince of peace always by your side. The prince of peace calms every stormy sea. He breathes peace into every troubled mind and His word brings reassurance of His promises of everlasting peace and joy. Therefore, never lose hope in God because He will never leave you nor abandon you, especially in the face of challenges.

PRAYER POINT:

Lord, guide me to always seek your face for in it I shall find peace.

Day 71

GOD KEEPS HIS PEOPLE

"You have granted me life and favor, and your care has preserved my spirit." -Job 10:12

Praise God, who is the giver of life. He is the Most High. Sing praises to him for He has given you and I life and had created us for His will and purpose only. God delights in His most precious creature-mankind. We are not just one of those but we are the very image and likeness of our father, God almighty.

The Almighty has chosen us to be called His own, so that freely, we might access Him in times of troubles or need. You are not a slave or a stranger to God. You are a child of God and you must always approach your father with that understanding. Now tell me, what would you think of a father, who never cares about his child's wellbeing? I bet it that you will call such a father all sorts of names like irresponsible, wicked, and heartless.

Surprisingly, the scripture confirms it this way;
"Can a woman forget her nursing child, and not have compassion on the son of her womb? Surely they may forget, yet I will not forget you." -Isaiah 49:15

Humans are limited in many ways. But God is the unlimited God. Regardless of what you do or not, He will never leave you to your destruction. Everything in God is good and perfect. There is no wickedness of any sort in God.

We have found favor in the sight of God and this is why we enjoy His goodness and mercy daily. The miracle of sleeping and waking is the underrated goodness of God. Always cherish the gift of every day because it is a reflection of God's goodness. God had dealt wondrously with us and we must show Him gratitude for all these things by giving Him thanks daily.

PRAYER POINT:
Dear Lord, I thank you for keeping me alive to see this day despite the challenges of life and my shortcomings. Thank you for all your love and care. I pray that you grant me the grace to love and obey you every day.

Day 72

HE IS OUR SAFETY

"The Lord is my rock and my fortress and my deliverer; My God, my strength, in whom I will trust; my shield and the horn of my salvation, my stronghold." -Psalms 18:2

Rock is a mass of stone projected out of the ground or water. Figuratively, a rock means something strong, stable, and dependable; a person who provides security or support to another. A fortress on its part is "a fortified place; a large and permanent fortification of a place.

With the above descriptions, God shows Himself to us as a place of protection and security, where every believer can run to in times of trouble. Like a rock, He is dependable and reliable. Nothing moves God. No situation makes Him fearful. You must begin to see yourself in God. He is the only secured place out of fear, anxiety, depression, and pain. If nothing can move God, then, no situation can displace you out of your position. You stand strong and firm in Him.

I realize that God was the first believer in Himself. He believes in His word when He called forth creation saying; let there be… (Genesis 1). God knows that His words will never fall to the ground empty until it fulfills the purpose for which He sent it. Similarly, He wants you and me to have this same firm assurance in Him just as He had demonstrated it at the beginning of creation.

Your faith in God keeps you secured in Him. Faith is to believe God to do the impossible even when all situation points to it that it can never be done. God wants you to have that unshakable and unmovable faith in Him today. He stands for those who stand in the assurance of His words. Believe God today and you will see Him do mighty things on your behalf.

PRAYER POINT:
Because you are my protector Lord, I come to you. Keep me safe from the plans of the devil.

Day 73

OBEDIENCE IS THE KEY TO HIS GOODNESS

If they obey and serve Him, They shall spend their days in prosperity, and their years in pleasures.
-Job 36:11

In the 36th Chapter of the book of Job from which the above verse was taken, Job's friend, Elihu proclaimed the goodness of God. He was consoling Job and given him reasons why he should not give up on God.

God is to be worshipped in obedience and love. He stated that those who obey the Lord shall spend their days in prosperity. God does not desert the righteous. He saves them from the bounds of the enemies. God opens our ears to hear his instructions so that we can follow them. He wants us to heed to His commanding and instructive voice, to attend to His admonitions, cautions, and follow them in humility. His blessings are for us.

There are dimensions of prosperity and pleasures that only open up as a result of obedience and service unto God. Meanwhile, the best show of obedience unto God is by obeying those He has placed in authority over us. Obedience and service unto God through men should not be dependent on our age and status; it should flow irrespective of whatever our situation is.

We serve God in men just as God blesses us through men. Brethren, we are being called today to obey God's words. Let us incline our ears to all His instructions irrespective of the channel or by what means such instruction comes. It is important to always remember that every of God's instructions through men must always be traceable to the Bible else such instruction becomes invalid.

PRAYER POINT:
Lord, help me to recognize that obedience to your words is most paramount in my life. May I always put you first in everything I do. Amen.

Day 74

HIS PEACE IS ENOUGH

I will both lie down in peace, and sleep; For You alone, O Lord, make me dwell in safety.
-Psalms 4:8

Babies and little children have nothing to worry about; all their needs are taken care of by their parents. No matter how big their requests may look, this peace assures them that all is well even when their parents are going through hard times. No one sleeps better than a man whose interest is assured in Christ. A mind that is free from worries, fear of every kind but full of peace and joy. Sleepless nights and restlessness are most times caused by the disordered or untrusting mind.

The protection of God is better than having a thousand armies surround you with guns. See the life of David in the Bible, he was a man after God's heart. It wasn't recorded that he had trouble sleeping despite having many enemies surround him. This is because the peace of God was his strength. Whoever has this has nothing to fear, and can sleep in peace like a newborn baby.

People around you may seek the things the world offers, but you must endeavor to run after God's favor and mercies. The Lord is full of righteousness. He is full of grace and mercy. So seek Him in prayers and love. Let the peace of God rock you to sleep. He who knows God and sleeps under his wings needs no other blanket nor pillow. He has nothing to fear, for no man can harm him. Come to Jesus today; let him take care of your needs. God is asking you to have faith in him, and he will take care of you. Allow God into your soul, and his peace will be with you.

PRAYER POINT:
Lord Jesus, I hand you the wheels of my life. Take care of my problems father, give me peace like you gave David. Amen.

HOW DO YOU HEAR?

"Therefore, take heed of how you hear...
Luke 8:18

This saying of Jesus came right after he spoke a parable of 'the sower and his seed,' The Lord instructs us in verse 18 to 'take heed how ye hear' in reference to the parables He had just told. How is it that we need to be warned about how we hear? The ear is a physical organ that is very vital for communication. The ear must be effective if there is to be good communication. The ear is the part of the body that connects you to God in the spirit realm. In the scripture many times the Lord would say, **"let him that has ears to hear, hear what the spirit is saying"** - Rev 3:22. God's plan for us is to hear and obey but the devil's plan is to intersect and interrupt our hearing so as not to obey.

Hearing is a major determinant of man's direction in life. According to the passage, the matter this time is not just hearing; it is HOW you hear. Anybody who has ears can hear, it will be ordinary sound if there is no positive action toward what was heard. How do you hear those things spoken physically and spiritually? What is your attitude to what you heard? Many hear with biased minds, some with uncertainty, some with uncared attitude, some with suspicion, and some with doubt. So, how they hear has been defective, hence their direction in life is faulty. James 1:9 teaches us to be quick to hear.

Let your attitude to hearing be quick. Hear with accuracy what God is saying. Hear completely what the spirit is saying to you. Put aside doubt, suspicion, bias, and all other things that are not of God. The cause of many issues of going the wrong direction, misunderstanding, and misinterpretation that has shattered many homes and lives have to do with how we hear. How you hear will determine where you will end up in life. Therefore, take heed of how you hear. Have this attitude to your hearing:
1. Be quick to hear,
2. Be accurate to hear,
3. Take heeds to details,
4. Her completely.

Above all. Let what you hear from God transform your life. You cannot remain the same after hearing. There must be a positive change in your life after hearing from God. Adapt to His word, do not hear, and remain the same. It shall be well with you in Jesus's name.

PRAYER:

Father, heal me of every hearing defect in the spirit that can hinder my progress. I plead the blood of Jesus over my ears on how I hear and follow through.

Day 76

GOD CARES

*"Casting all your care upon Him,
for He cares for you." -1 Peter 5:7*

What a joy when someone is readily available to give you care when you need it the most. The same way someone else feels when you show some love and care. However, you are over joyous when God shows you his care.

Many times, when people pray to God, they do not place their entire burden on God, they still pity God and carry some of the prayed burdens. You really must be a good caregiver here-helping God to carry your burden. Well, we have a God that is so mighty, and your burden to him is less than a pint so that he can carry them. However, you should learn to trust and surrender all to him.

The text says; casting all your care upon Him; involves both showing your love to God and surrendering your burden to God because he cares for you. He can take care of you. He single-handedly takes care of all the animals and trees, how much more we his children who were created by him and for him.

Don't let the weight of life pull you down, release all to God, and see him taking you higher.

PRAYER POINT:
Father, in the name of Jesus, I release all to you, and I begin to enjoy your care, amen.

Day 77

LIGHT UP

***"The spirit of a man is the lamp of the Lord,
searching all the inner depths of his heart."***
-Proverbs 20:27

Have you tried entering a room and moving about in the room without the lights on and still not fall or hit your legs and head? The power of light cannot be over-emphasis as its benefits are more than the light itself.

The Holy Spirit interacts with our spirit man to make us a better person. A believer without the fullness of the Holy Spirit will have difficulty in his Christian faith, as the Holy Spirit can reveal deep and hidden things unknown to men. Whenever you need more in-depth light on someone, the business you want to undergo, or even what will happen ahead, the Holy Spirit can tell you.

Are you at a crossroad and you needing direction? You may need to talk to the Holy Spirit before you make that decision.

160

He will give you the best option because he can see ahead of us. The Holy Spirit is inexhaustible; you can get more of him

PRAYER POINT:

Father in the name of Jesus, I receive the Spirit of God. Amen

Day 78

KEEP IT LOW

"By humility and the fear of the LORD are riches, honor and life." -Proverbs 22:4

Amazing how you hear your name called out as the best for the year among many contenders who are more qualified than you. It's great to celebrate and have fun. Whenever you are getting such accolades or achievements, you should have a control measure that will keep you in check to avoid pride. Nothing stops you from being rich or achieving great things in life and yet not bragging about it or being full of yourself. Be humble, keep it low, quietly be rich, and become great without noise.

PRAYER POINT:

Father in the name of Jesus, I receive the spirit of humility; help me never to become proud at any point in my life, Amen.

Day 79

WE WANT TO UNDERSTAND

For you are bringing some strange things to our ears. Therefore we want to know what these things mean." -Acts 17:20

As Christians, it is our duty always to preach the word of God everywhere we find ourselves and at every point in time. If we read this chapter from the very beginning, we will understand that Paul and Silas who passed through Amphipolis and Apollonian came to Thessalonica where they "argued" the scriptures, explaining them and quoting passages which proclaimed Christ the Messiah. Some believed and the unbelieving created an uprising to capture Paul and Silas. They then escape to Beroea to continue to preach the word of God. Those here were better disposed and many believed and repented but the Thessalonians came and caused them to leave once again. This time they went to Athens where they argued with philosophers and then in Areopagus, they were asked to explain those strange things they have set forth.

These men were known for saying and hearing new things. They were ready to add to their wealth of knowledge in religious study and it will take great power and spiritual wisdom on Paul not to just preach as usual but to harvest souls for Christ. As a believer, there will be times when you will have to defend your faith and justify your beliefs both to believers and unbelievers alike. To the ignorant and the highly educated. The truth is that men want to know about our faith. They want to know about God. Far beyond the benefits of salvation which include prosperity, riches, promotion, and others, are you equipped enough to convince a very rich man that he needs God? Some of our prayer points are daily realities for some men, how then can you convince them that they need God?

The gospel is the power of God unto salvation for Greece and gentiles. May the Lord help us individually to know the saving power of the gospel and to wear it like armor to pull down the stronghold in the heart of men by publishing this gospel.

PRAYER POINT:

Lord, give me the grace to be able to preach your word to both the ignorant and educated and lead them to the right. Amen.

Day 80

CHILD OF GOD

"Beloved, now we are children of God; and it has not been revealed what we shall be, but we know that when He is revealed, we shall be like Him, for we shall see Him as He is" -I John 3:2

When you speak ill of another, you are not different from the guy who shot the same person with a gun. The worst case will be when you are the shooter and the victim. Whenever, you look down on yourself, speak negative words into your life, always staying on the wrong mindset, shooting yourself.

Never let anyone call you who you are not and don't attempt to change what God calls you. If you keep calling yourself a failure, that's exactly who you will become irrespective of your present status. However, if you begin with a personal confession of our text;

"Your name", Now I am a child of God for it has not yet been revealed what I shall be but I have the confidence that I will know when He is revealed, I shall be like Him, for I shall see Him as He is.

Keep confessing until you become a reality of your words.

PRAYER POINT:

Father, in the name of Jesus, I declare I am your child, I become like You Lord, Amen.

Day 81

UNWAVERING TRUST

"Whenever I am afraid, I will trust in you"
- Psalm 56:3

Whenever a child is in danger, and he sighted his mother, he calls out to her which depicts the child trusted his Mother to save him. On the sound of his voice, his mother by default rushes to save him using all necessary and available tools this and much more can God do most especially when we trusted him wholeheartedly.

When you are going through trouble, what do you do? Do you complain, pass blame, or put your trust in God? The Psalmist says; whenever I am afraid, I will trust in you. Trusting God, especially in trials shows to God you don't have any other option, your plan A is God, your plan B is God, your plan C is God.

A songwriter says;
I will trust you in Jesus, I will trust in you, I will follow you till I see you face to face.
Where lays your trust in good and bad times?

PRAYER POINT:

Father, in the name of Jesus, I will keep on trusting you, help me Lord in my trials, help me Lord not to lose faith in you. Amen.

Day 82

GOODNESS

*"For the Lord is good; His mercy is everlasting,
and His truth endures to all generations."*
-Psalm 100:5

Driving towards the hills, he saw from afar off a woman soaked in the rain waving and shouting; he was contemplating whether to stop and be of help or drive past from the risk of being robbed. After much trouble in his mind, he finally pulled over after driving past some meters. He reversed and winded down the glass. The woman was crying and was able to mutter; "there is a ditch ahead, don't go that way". The man ran down with an umbrella and a coat to bring her into the vehicle. Upon settling in, the man burst into tears, and all he could mutter was; thank you, thank you.

Every time, God shows and pours his goodness upon us, only a few recognize them. The Lord wishes to save the man, hence, he planted the woman at that point irrespective of the condition. He could have chosen to drive off, but for a second thought of showing mercy and being good to the woman, he got a reward for that this action. The Lord is good and in turn, wants us to show mercy to everyone around.

<h3 style="text-align:center">PRAYER POINT:</h3>

Father, in the name of Jesus, thank you, Lord for showing me your goodness, helps me Lord to extend this goodness to others without looking back.

Day 83

THE COUNSEL OF THE WICKED

An evildoer gives heed to false lips; a liar listens eagerly to a spiteful tongue. -Proverbs 17:4

"Show me your friends and I will tell you who you are" is a popular saying. Our lives are greatly influenced by the lifestyles of the friends we keep. A lot of people doubt this and argue that we can keep friends from any sphere of life and still not be influenced by their way of life. This however is a fallacy. How can you spend time with people, discuss with them, take their advice, run to them in times of need, and say that their lives do not influence yours?

The influence of the company we keep cannot be overemphasized. In the above Bible verse, it states that the evildoer gives heed to false lips and a liar listens eagerly to a spiteful tongue. If we do not want to join this set of people then we need to be careful of the company we keep and the people we solicit advice from. If you keep bad company, subconsciously you learn their behavior and attitudes. We need to constantly be in prayer so as not to fall to the

171

temptation of joining a bad company that will lead us astray and far away from the presence of God.

We also need to be wary of the advice we listen to and very conscious of the ones we choose as a partner. Never forget that God is the greatest adviser. He is the greatest friend. He is the best company you should keep. Spend time with God by meditating on his words every day and he will guide you.

PRAYER POINT:
Father, I have no powers on my own so I trust your judgment completely. Give me the grace to choose my friends wisely that I may never stray from the path of light. Amen.

Day 84

GO UP AT ONCE

*"Then Caleb quieted the people before Moses,
and said; Let us go up at once and take possession,
for we are well able to overcome it." -Numbers 13:30*

Successful people grab at once when they see opportunities. If you want to go far in life, you not only need to take the risk but grab and take risks that are worth launching you into the next level. It may look not the right step to take, but as long as you have an assurance of peace and, you can see the future in it, go for it.

Go up at once at the right time; if you fail to take that decision now, you may end up paying dearly for it as the children of Israel did in Numbers 14: 40-45. Just like you have departure time for trains and airplanes, there is always a right time for everything; you cannot afford to miss it.

You are at the point of making a tough decision which has either a positive or negative side to it, consult the Holy Spirit,

173

and if there is a green light on either of the two, do not hesitate to march on, for your victory is now.

PRAYER POINT:

Father in the name of Jesus, I receive grace and strength to put into action what I need to do quickly at the right time, Amen.

Day 85

HE FULFILLS HIS PROMISES

*May the Lord give you increase more and more,
you and your children. -Psalms 115:14*

Praise be to God, the giver of everything beautiful. May his name be exalted for he is the Lord. He is the King of Kings, the Lord of Lords, and the Most High God who reigns forever. His Kingdom is everlasting. His reign has no end. No one can stand before Him. The devil trembles at His voice. The Lord never changes, He is the same yesterday, today, and forever. He is full of promises. Unlike men, he does not promise and fail. All he says he does. He never leaves the people who love and worships him.

Are you having a hard time right now? Are things not going as you planned them? You do not have enough to feed your family? You are finding it hard to cater to their needs? You cannot afford to pay your bills? You cannot take care of your family's health? No one has it all. Life is a mixture of the good, the bad, and the ugly. At times it brings the good to us and other times it comes with the bad. Sometimes it leaves us empty, devastated, and worn out. Doubts of God's mercy creeps in. Is he still there? we ask. He made promises, is he still going to fulfill them or should we find alternative negative means?

Brethren, relax, for what God is preparing for you is greater beyond your imaginations. What you should keep in mind is that God does not operate with our own time. He operates in his own time. A thousand days in our eyes is like a moment before God. He has promised to give you more and more increase and he will fulfill it. His grace continues and he never fails. This promise he extends to your children and to even your future generations. Take a seat and wait for God's blessings, they are closer to fulfillment than you think.

PRAYER POINT:
Lord, give me the grace to wait for the fulfillment of your promises. May I not be carried away by the things of the world. Amen.

Day 86

I SHALL LIVE

**_I shall not die, but live, and declare
the works of the Lord._**   *-Psalms 118:17*

The tongue is but a little member of the body but it boasts great things (James 3:5). Jesus Christ taught that the tongue reflects the content of the heart. What you feel about yourself irrespective of whatever you are going through can only be known by the expression from your mouth. David in Psalm 118 highlighted how enduring God's mercy is. He was surrounded by many fears and death was close but he declared in the midst of all that he will not die. Today I make positive declarations in your life. Untimely death shall never know you. The eyes of the wicked shall never see you. Accidents are not your portion. You shall live.

A farmer planted the seed of the same quality and source in two different bowls. He separated them like 20m away from each other but supplied the same nutrient in quality and quality. Every morning after watering the two bowls, he blesses one with all blessings on fruitfulness and curses the second. After four weeks of blessing and cursing the bowls of seed, the first with a blessing was seen to be very green, healthy, bearing fruits while the second though with the same quality and nutrient was seen with withered leaves, stunted growth, and unpleasant to behold. Today, God wants you to know that there is power in the tongue. What you say is what shall come to pass. So you to cultivate the habit of speaking positive words to yourself every day.

You can do this in the morning after your morning prayers or devotion. Being rest assured that God hears you every time. He shall hear these words and bring them into fulfillment. Things around you may be so discouraging and may not be palatable, yet make it your daily duty to always declare good things to yourself. David was faced with death but he declared he will live for God's glory. Make bold your declaration and let the devil know that you have not subjected your life to be defined by your present situation.

PRAYER POINT:
Today I speak positivity into my life. Keep me, safe Lord. Keep me alive Father. May I live to proclaim your goodness to all of humanity. Amen.

Day 87

ASK ALWAYS, HE ANSWERS

Ask, and it will be given to you; seek, and you will find; knock, and it will be opened to you.
-Matthew 7:7

Sometimes we find it difficult to ask our friends or relatives for help whenever we need it. How would they react? Will they help us or will they make excuses? All these questions and such likes to run through our minds at every crossroad. The fear of not getting what we asked for makes us keep mute most times. However, we often feel disappointed when we see our friends give out the same things we would have asked for to others who requested them.

Our relationship with God is similar to that of our earthly relatives and friends. Even though God sees that you need some things, He would want you to ask them before He gives you. You will not be so free to ask your father about anything when you are not interested in building a relationship with him. This means that relationship precedes asking. God is

179

interested in having a relationship with you as His son. So He wants you to ask to receive, seek to find, and to knock before the door will be opened. God is extending His hands of fellowship to you, will you embrace it?

Don't forget that He knows our every need even before we were born. He is aware of what we need now or what we will need in the future. However, that effort of seeking that which you want is what God wants to see. So whatever you need, ask God for it and be rest assured that He will supply it. No need to look for help elsewhere when you have God. If earthly fathers will respond to the needs of their children, how much more our heavenly Father who fathers all fathers.

PRAYER POINT:
Dear Lord, I come to you today with all my needs knowing that you will answer and provide them all. Help me to trust in your divine providence. Amen.

Day 88

WHO HOLDS THE ROD?

"For this reason I also suffer these things; nevertheless I am not ashamed, for I know whom I have believed and am persuaded that He is able to keep what I have committed to Him until that Day." -2 Timothy 1:12

The understanding of who holds you in all of these things matters to your standing. The rod only responds to the power of the holder. Moses' rod was an ordinary rod in the hand of any other person than himself and Aaron. If Joshua or Caleb had used the rod, it would have meant nothing to them. But because of the grace and anointing upon Moses and the power of God, whenever he used the rod, something wonderful happened. This means that whatever the rod would become could be directed and ensured by the holder of it.

Likewise, as the LORD holds you, He oversees what you become in life. You are not to be afraid of what will become of your life; God directs your paths. The future is no news to your Heavenly Father. He knows what He is making out of your entire experiences, and He will see to it that you become what He intends you to be.

However, you need to trust Him as Paul did, and as Jesus did when He walked the earth. You need to see Him as a responsible Father that will not leave you amid confusion and walk away. Jesus promised that he would never leave us as orphans in the world and so He sent his Holy Spirit to us to dwell in us and with us. This is to ensure that there's no time that you are uncovered. He holds you and leads you on in the path of righteousness and prosperity.

It is not where you are dropped or how you are dropped that matters most but who dropped you there. For God will not leave you or forsake you in the smoke of affliction and pretend as if nothing is happening to you; after a short while, He will come and pick you up again, and the miraculous is bound to have happened in your life.

PRAYER POINT:
Lord, I thank you for holding me and directing my paths. I believe in what you are doing with my life, and I pray that you show me your ways that I may trust you the more.

Day 89

YOUR DAY OF RESTORATION HAS COME

So I will restore to you the years that the swarming locust has eaten, the crawling locust, the consuming locust, and the chewing locust, my great army which I sent among you. You shall eat in plenty and be satisfied, and praise the name of the Lord your God, Who has dealt wondrously with you; and my people shall never be put to shame. -Joel 2:25-26

Praise the Lord. Our time of restoration has come, and we shall praise His name. It sometimes appears that Christians are the ones suffering and going through difficulties while unbelievers seem to be enjoying all the benefits of life. The devil seems to be investing so much of resources into the life of unbelievers to taunt us and to keep them remained in darkness. Believers, on the other hand, are faced with many delays and denials to try our faith and bring us into the kingdom. Act 14:22.

In academics, those who engage in examination malpractices get a better grade than those who burned the midnight candle. In our business and places of work, it seems that those who engage in corruption, embezzlement, and cut corners are the ones who succeed and get promotion leaving the righteous behind. It sometimes seems like all the things God promised us are just vague and unrealistic. Time goes, and yet things remain unchanged. Four years is gone, and nothing new seems to have happened to you. The pressure is getting increased from friends and families as they expect that your faith should have delivered the long-awaited testimony.

Your delays are not denials. God will help you and that He will do at the right time. God's promise for you today is to restore the years that have been eaten up by the circumstances and challenges in your life. When the Lord shall restore your captivity, it will be like they never existed. Or have you ever seen the righteous forsaken? What makes you feel that God has forgotten you? He will not, His word for you today is restoration. You shall eat and be satisfied. While you wait for Him to come, don't worry about anything; just let your prayers, supplications, and thanksgiving bring your request to God.

PRAYER POINT:
O Lord, I decree that I reap all the harvest you promised me. I take back everything the devil stole from me and I rejoice always. Amen.

Day 90

HIS MERCY PROTECTS US

Through the Lord's mercies we are not consumed, because His compassions fail not.
-Lamentations 3:2

The fierceness and the heat from the sun alone are enough to consume all of humanity. God had in time, past used rain to wipe off the human race. We are not yet consumed because of His tender mercies towards us. Praise be to the ever merciful and compassionate God. He is compassionate towards the sheep of His pasture. His compassion knows no end, and his mercies endure forever.

If God were to judge or destroy us based on our sins, we all must have been dead by now. Many times, we are even proud to repent and turn from our wicked ways, yet in compassion, He looks away from our iniquity. God is so optimistic about us that He believes so much that we will bring Him glory and honor. There are many traps that the devil has set on our way. We do not even know many of these lest we pray against them. Yet God in His mercy preserves us from them all. We will appreciate this mercy more if we are aware of many battles God fights behind us that we don't even know.

God is compassionate. He understands our humanness. He knows that we are weak, and we need him to overcome the power of sin. He will not allow us to be consumed by sin, the fire, the storm, the crisis, the infections, the chaos, and even tribulations we find ourselves. We need to always thank him for the unfailing mercy and compassion he showers on us each day.

PRAYER POINT:

O merciful Father, thank you for your constant mercy and compassion over me, may I never think less of how merciful you are to me always. Amen

Day 91

HIS MERCY IS SUFFICIENT

Oh, satisfy us early with your mercy that we may rejoice and be glad all our days. Make us glad according to the days in which you have afflicted us, the years in which we have seen evil.
-Psalms 90:14-15

The mercy of God is everlasting. He looks on pity on those who turn to Him for mercy. Our father is ever-loving, ever forgiving. He is ever merciful, ever powerful. Though he allows the devil to tempt us, he never really leaves us alone.

We should not underestimate the mercies of God. We should always be prayerful and ask God for his mercies upon us. As humans, we sin unknowingly and inadvertently. We might not know when we commit these sins. In our daily life, we sin knowingly and unknowingly.

If we screen our every thought bought the conscious and subconscious ones, then we would be surprised at the number of sins we commit just by our thoughts alone. Our brain is always at work, and we do not always consciously control thought of malice, envy, jealousy, pride, or anger.

His lovingkindness is always with us, and we are his children. He cannot forsake us. He will shower us with mercy first thing in the morning so that we have a deposit of his mercies to withdraw from for every unbidden sin we might commit in the course of the day. That notwithstanding, we should guard our hearts so that it will not be filled with evil thoughts. Because from the abundance of the heart, the mouth speaks.

PRAYER POINT:

Father, satisfy us early with your mercy. Give us the joy that can only come from you that we may leave a life that is pleasing to you. Amen.

Day 92

GUARD YOUR HEART

"KEEP vigilant watch over your heart; that's where life starts." -Proverbs 4:23

If you have allowed the thoughts of death to prevail in your heart, then your body will soon die. If you have been full of thoughts of danger and fear, then danger will soon reach you. Whatever you fill your heart with will surely be drawn to you. That's why you need to guard your heart with all sense of diligence.

Your heart is like the palace of a king who rules over a kingdom. It is the most important place in the kingdom because that's where the king lives and sits to make decisions that matter to the kingdom. That is where the highest authority in the kingdom lies. If any enemy captures the land, he must first attack the palace of the king and make sure the palace is subdued; then he can go ahead to take the whole kingdom. If the devil takes charge of your experiences, he will advance against your heart through thoughts that weaken faith. And you must gird your heart against such.

When you go through a time of need, he whispers to you that you are a poor person and will die poor. When you feel sick in your body, he comes to tell you that you are suffering from one sin or the other. He comes with condemnations and explanations. He brings guilt and self-pity which is never from God to your heart so that you can lose your faith and begin to meditate on his words. It is a strategy to rip you off of your armor and strength in the promise of the Lord. You must not allow that.

Now, how do you guard your heart against the devil and unclean influences? It is by the word of God. This you will see in the following lesson. For today, your attention is to be drawn towards the importance of your heart in the whole issue of your life. For which if care is not taken, it becomes the source of death and failure which are never from God.

PRAYER POINT:

Dear Lord, I see that my heart has a lot to do with my well-being; I now pray that you take over all my heart and keep me in your will always in Jesus's name.

Day 93

TEAR THEM DOWN

"Casting down arguments and every high thing that exalts itself against the knowledge of God, bringing every thought into captivity to the obedience of Christ." *-2Corinthians 10:5*

You are responsible for the thoughts that prevail in your heart. As you have understood that life or death begins in the heart, whatever you allow to win your thought, wins your entire life. Whatever you see through the eyes of your heart becomes the reality you have. No man can help you if your heart does not help you. And now you have been given the responsibility to get serious with everything that settles in your heart. You determine what stays and what does not stay.

If it doesn't match what God's word has said to you, you tear it down. Now, to tear it down signifies that it is like a structure or a building of some kind. Yes, every thought you allow to stay in your heart becomes part of a structure that's in your heart. Your heart is a large field that is considered suitable for great structures, and there are only three interested builders; the LORD, Satan, and man. These three take great interest in building some great structures in your heart for a purpose.

They all build through words—spoken or written. God speaks to your good and peace and edification, but Satan and men speak to their selfish interest and your destruction. And that's why you must tear down every structure men has raised in your heart by counsel and pity. It is not of God. You tear them down by the word of God.

You don't answer the devil by your explanations or discussions but by the word of God. Every part of life has been provided for in the word of God and when you find it out, attack the ideas from hell. The word of God will surely prevail over all other words if you raise it above all.

There are several ways you speak the word: in confession and proclamation, in prayers and songs. You speak the word of God aloud to yourself until you are convinced of its truth and its surety.

PRAYER POINT:
My God, I believe in your word, and I know that my heart is a field. I pray that as from today; help me never to allow the words of Satan or men to tear down your word in me. Amen.

# Day 94

GOD IS ALL YOU NEED

The Spirit of God has made me, and the breath of the Almighty gives me life. -Job 33:4

Part of the mistake most people make in life is to search for alternatives to God. You are alive. You can walk. Your eyes are working perfectly well. You can breathe freely through your nose. You hear everything said. What's more? You can afford three square meals a day. You have your fleet of cars. You have numerous houses. Life is perfect. What is an ideal life without God? Imperfect. Incomplete. Something is missing.

Let me ask you whose spirit is in you? Who is your creator? Who made you? Who is the reason why you are still breathing? God is the giver of life and everything beautiful. In him, all things were made. No one can have anything unless he wills it. Your wealth, money, cars, mansions, beautiful clothes, and expensive jewelry, all these things can be taken away from you in the twinkle of an eye. It all takes a snap of fingers; everything will vanish.

What then will happen to you if you do not abide in God? Do you remember the story of Job in the Bible? Job had all the good things of life, the clothes, the jewelry, the gold, the houses, large livestock, and children. He was a very wealthy man. Despite his wealth, he served God with all his heart. Taking permission from God, the devil came to try Job. He took away everything that Job had, absolutely everything. His wife advised him to curse God and die. Even his faithful friends left him at some point. But Job never wavered. He stood firm on his faith. God restored everything he lost in ten folds because he showed strong faith in the almighty.

Are you worshiping God because your life is blissful now? What happens when trials come? Will you still stand firm? Remember that everything in the world is just passing away. God is the only constant thing. His arms are always wide open, waiting to welcome you. Never forget that it is his breath that gives you life. You do not need wealth; you need God. You will have all the other good things of life in abundance when you worship the Lord because he gives every good thing of life in abundance.

PRAYER POINT:
Dear Lord, Help me today to understand that you are the giver of life and that your words are true. May I never stray from the path of righteousness. Amen.

Day 95

LEARN TO PRAY

"Now it came to pass, as he was praying in a certain place when he ceased, that one of his disciples said to him, 'Lord, teach us to pray, as John also taught his disciples.'" -*Luke 11:1*

Prayer is both an art and a conversation. It is an act because it is a practice by man to relate with a deity or a superior humbly, to obtain what is desired by him. It is a conversation because man expects to have a reply from the deity either in words or in materials, or a feeling. In any way, prayer is a connection between the physical realm and the spirit realm.

As a believer, the first thing you need to know about prayer is that you don't know how to pray that will produce an effective result. You surely know that you have a need in your heart and sometimes you can explain and at other times, you cannot. Because of the limitation of your mind, you need the help of the Holy Spirit to pray the right prayers.

The disciples came to Jesus, wanting to understand how to pray and when to pray. They have seen Jesus pray for hours nonstop, and they wondered what he always said and how he could have much to say. They doubtlessly knew whom He was praying to, but they were confused on how the prayer went always. So they approached him to teach them to pray. At times you don't even know you should pray because you are unaware of what is going on in the spirit. Until the disciples saw the need to learn to pray, they could not do much talking with God. They have been talking but not with God. It is quite possible for you to keep talking and explaining your needs but not praying. Until you have been taught to pray by the Holy Spirit, you will never be able to pray aright. You will see later how the Holy Spirit teaches us to pray now that Jesus is no longer physically on the earth to teach us.

PRAYER POINT:
Lord Jesus, teach me to pray.

THE TWO REALMS OF PRAYING

"But you, beloved, building yourselves up on your most holy faith, praying in the Holy Spirit."
-Jude 1:20

There are two realms of praying: the realm of the flesh and the realm of the Spirit. The realm in which you pray will determine the result you obtain and from whom you obtain it. As a child of God, you have been called into the realm and domain of the Christ—the Holy Spirit. You are no longer to walk, think or pray after the flesh—its lust, passion, wants, and everything that draws away from the will of the Father.

The realm in which you pray tells of the source of your prayer power; that is sponsoring your words or content of your prayer. Now, doing a careful review of all your prayers before now, can you find out where they came from and from whom they originated? Are they not of the flesh? Or are they of the Spirit? You must know that what is of the flesh is not always obvious or detectable except as revealed by the Holy Spirit. However, one thing is certain of the prayers sponsored by the flesh: it is never submissive to the will of God. It puts oneself first, others next, and God last. It is a prayer made in partnership with the will of the devil—secretly.

The realm in which you pray is the generator of your words in prayer. You may appear to be praying to God, but the source of your words and desires will decide what you are doing. The flesh is always in partnership with and in submission to the devil, sin, and death.

But to pray in the Holy Spirit is to be empowered by the Holy Spirit. It is to say words that are generated in the heart of the Holy Spirit inside of you (Romans 8:27). He directs your thoughts and desires in prayers in partnership with and in submission to the will of the Father, unto whom you have come. How can you be in the Holy Spirit when you pray? It is by meditating always and regularly in the Word of God—the words of the Bible as inspired by the Holy Spirit. It is the Word of God in your heart that positions you in the Holy Spirit in prayer. Can you see how much less can be done when you pray in the flesh?

PRAYER POINT:
Thank you, father, for the Holy Spirit in me. I submit to His will and believe in the name of Jesus that as from today, as I meditate in the word of God, I will pray in the Holy Spirit and not in the flesh.

Day 97

THE TOOLS OF PRAYERS
(PART ONE)

"Therefore let him who speaks in a tongue pray that he may interpret. For if I pray in a tongue, my spirit prays, but my understanding is unfruitful. What is the conclusion then? I will pray with the spirit, and I will also pray with the understanding. I will sing with the spirit, and I will also sing with the understanding." - 1 Corinthians 14:13-15

In the last teaching, you saw that there are two realms of praying: in the flesh and the Spirit. And now you will see the two tools of praying. From the bible passage above, it is revealed that a believer can pray with his spirit and he can pray with his mind as well. Both are acceptable to God and effectual. The two realms of praying are the generators, while the two tools are the carriers or the transporters of prayers.

To pray with the spirit is another way to say you pray in other tongues. You don't understand what you are saying by any

199

natural means; a supernatural way also interprets a natural way. However, it is the highway of the spirit, a path where no devil threads successfully. It is the path that no witch or demons can find. It is the secured channel of communication with the Lord. Nevertheless, it is only communication between your spirit and God. Your understanding does not increase, and you know nothing of what you are saying.

But you are an intelligent being, and you need your mind to be involved in whatever will be done in this world. So you will need to use your understanding also in praying. As you pray in tongues, you set your mind on the words that the Spirit speaks into your mind, and you speak them out in your understanding. It may be scripture or a prayer point or a declaration or a song, that's the interpretation of your tongues. It is to give your mind a direction after the will of the Father. Learn to pray with both your spirit and your mind.

PRAYER POINT:
In the name of Jesus, I pray with my spirit and with my mind according to the will of the father. Amen.

Day 98

THE TOOLS OF PRAYER
(PART TWO)

"He who speaks in a tongue edifies himself,
but he who prophesies edifies the church."
-1 Corinthians 14:4

While a believer prays with his spirit, something happens to him from within. He is being changed. He is being pruned and cleaned. Every dross that has laid hold of his mind begins to drop off as he continues in prayers; because what is from above is above all. The language of the spirit is supernatural and transcendent to the language of the earth. When, as a believer, you begin to pray in other tongues, you subject your mind to a repair process, and an adjustment is being made in your entire being to the glory of God. As you pray in tongues, you attract the people of like passion—the angels of God, to come and do business with you. As you pray in other tongues, you repel the people of unlike passions—the devil and unclean spirits.

It is a way to adjust your spiritual atmosphere here on earth. It is the highway to take your soul and body to where your spirit is in Christ in heavenly places. As you keep on praying in the power of the Holy Spirit, you put all things in their places as they were in the beginning—under the dominion of man.

PRAYER POINT:

In the name of Jesus, I pray in other tongues by the power of the Holy Spirit, and I interpret in the common language of the around me as needed. Thank you, Father, for all you have given me through Christ.

Day 99

PRAY WITH ALL KINDS OF PRAYER

***"Praying always with all prayer and supplication
in the Spirit, being watchful to this end with all
perseverance and supplication for all the saints."***
-Ephesians 6:18

There are different kinds of prayer that you can pray. And there are different ways that you can pray. The Bible is full of prayers said by many people and in different ways. A number of them are thanksgiving, petition, supplication, intercession, proclamation or declaration, etc. so many believers only know how to request from the Lord without knowing how to do other forms of prayer. And without other kinds of prayer, your prayer life will not be robust and effective. It is your responsibility to find out how to pray that will be effective and not just waste your time changing nothing.

You will see now and later, that there are different ways to pray and different prayers to say. There are different levels of prayer that you will need to engage for you to get better results through prayers.

203

You will recall that there are only two realms of praying and two tools of praying. You are a believer, and it is expected of you to pray in the Spirit and to pray with your spirit and with your mind. But now that you are in the spirit and with the tools of praying, you will make use of the tools at different levels of prayers. There are three levels of prayer, as described in Matthew 7:7 and Luke 11:9. They are asking, seeking, and knocking.

When you don't ask when you are to ask, you will not receive. When you don't seek when you are to seek, you will not find, and finally, when you don't knock at a closed-door, it is not opened unto you. You will see how to engage these different levels of prayers in the following teaching.

PRAYER POINT:

Father, I thank you for the different ways you have given to me to pray to you. I pray that you grant me all the wisdom to engage the right kind of prayers when I need to in Jesus's name.

$\mathcal{D}ay$ 100

ASK, AND YOU WILL RECEIVE

"So I say to you ask, and it will be given to you..." -Matthew 7:7

To ask is not to seek and it is not to knock. To ask is to approach God as a Father that gives. In asking, you expect to receive, and you know what you are asking for exactly. It is the lowest level and the simplest level of all the three—asking, seeking, and knocking. You speak to God in your precise understanding, asking that He gives you what you know He is eager to give. As explained earlier, when you ask, you must expect to receive.

To ask is to place a demand on God based on your understanding that He has what you are demanding. If you don't know or you are not convinced that he has what you are asking, you eventually do not receive because you are not asking in faith. Faith is the conviction that God has what He gives and gives what He has to his children. As a believer, you are to ask God only according to His will as revealed in the Word of God and directed by the Holy Spirit.

Asking has a purpose. Jesus said in John 16:24, "until now you have asked nothing in my name. Ask, and you will receive that your joy may be full." The purpose of asking is fulfilled in our joy being full in the Holy Ghost. God gives us what we ask of Him because He sincerely wants our joy to be full. Whenever you approach God, in His will, to ask for whatever thing, have it in mind that He delights in giving things to His children so that your joy will be full. He is not interested in your pain and tears and frustration. He is neither interested in you having sorrow day and night.

Asking has a promise. Jesus said again, "...ask, and it will be given unto you." The Lord Jesus Christ has given you His unfailing word on asking. You will certainly receive what you ask in Jesus's name. However, asking is precise and understood by both man and God. You don't ask from God without your mind involved. In other words, you don't ask by praying in tongues. You ask in the language you understand and in faith in the name of Jesus.

PRAYER POINT:

Father, I thank you today for the purpose and the promise of asking in the name of Jesus. I know that you hear me and do what I ask in Jesus's name.

Day 101

SEEK, AND YOU SHALL FIND

"Or what woman, having ten silver coins, if she loses one coin, does not light a lamp, sweep the house, and search carefully until she finds it? And when she has found it, she calls her friends and neighbors together, saying, 'Rejoice with me, for I have found the piece which I lost!" - Luke 15:8-9

To seek is higher than to ask. Asking takes a posture of saying what you need and demanding that it is given to you as to when due; but seeking involves your moves, your participation in the whole thing. The scripture above describes a woman who loses one of her ten coins and who will not forget it altogether. She keeps the remaining nine somewhere and goes about to seek out the tenth coin. She sweeps out every corner to see that all is open to her eyes. She checks here and there, and until she finds it, she does not stop searching. While she's searching, she will be asking too. If she has a relative around, she will ask him or her if the coin was found somewhere. You can imagine what happens when you lose a thousand dollar note out of five thousand dollars. You will search and ask until you find it.

This illustration reveals that seeking is intentional and directed. It has a purpose too: So that your joy may be full. Until you have found what you are seeking, you have not succeeded in it. You don't seek by daydreaming or by wishing. You stand up and bend over or kneel to search out every corner of your heart and of the word of God to find the will of God. You get involved in it. You sit down and study the scripture, asking questions as you study. It is deliberate and hard work.

PRAYER POINT:
My God, thank you for the gift of the Word of God that has given us a way to seek out things in the kingdom. I pray that through your Holy Spirit, I will learn to seek to find in Jesus's name.

Day 102

IN HIM YOU SHALL FIND STRENGTH

He gives power to the weak, And to those who have no might, He increases strength.
-Isaiah 40:29

You are tired, lost, nothing went as planned, and everything is over. Your heart is heavy because you lost your job, lost your loved one. Or peradventure, you are down with sickness, everything is bleak, and nothing seems to be working. You have been stable for a long; finally, all the stress overwhelmed you. Life has not been what you expected it to be. When you were younger, you had a picture of how perfect you want your life to be. Now that you are an adult, that picture has become nothing but a memory. Everything is supposed to be great, you wish. You keep trying, but it seems not just working out. You break down., drown your pillow with tears and about to give up. It's all right. At one point in our lives, we have all been there. That is why we need the Almighty God; to our rescue on the days, the world turns against us.

God is the only one who strengthens those who are weak. He consoles the afflicted. Father of those who fatherless, mother of those who is motherless. He keeps the orphan safe, the companion to those who have no one. He is calling you by your name. Come to me and find strength, come to me, and I will make you strong again. Stronger than you will ever be.

How many times do you call on God? How many times do you talk with him? If you do not often have a heart to heart talk with God, our father, then start now. He is calling you back to him. He wishes to help you get through the trials and worries of life. Come with your sorrows and pains. Drop them all at his feet. He is asking you today to lean on him. Let him help you. Life can be overwhelming, but in him alone, you can draw strength to continue the journey of life.

PRAYER POINT:

Lord, I am only human full of weakness. I acknowledge that in you alone, I will find strength. Give me the strength to endure all the trials of life, and may I praise you through it all. Amen.

Day 103

NUMEROUS BLESSINGS

Many, O Lord my God, are Your wonderful works Which You have done; And Your thoughts toward us Cannot be recounted to You in order; If I would declare and speak of them, They are more than can be numbered. -Psalms 40:5

The name of the Lord be praised forever. Let the heavens and earth exalt his holy name, and the birds of the air sing him praises. The Lord is faithful and kind. He keeps all that he has promised. Beautiful are the works of his hand. Marvelous are the things he has done for us.

How do you define God when things are tough? Many only call God a good God when things are so sweet and rosy. Their definition of God falls apart when things fall apart. Some will even curse him at the slightest chance they have. Why will evil befall me if truly he cares? Where was he when this or that happened? Couldn't he have stopped me from losing those things I lost? David thought of God's faithfulness and declared that His ways are perfect, his words are tried, and that he is a shield to those who trust in him (Psalm 30:18).

Just to remind you a few of all God has done, He has kept you safe from the evil one. He has blinded their eyes to your success. He has hidden you under his shadow, protected you from harm. The Lord has filled your paths with light. His thoughts towards you are good. All he wishes for you is great. He does not want you to be lost. The Lord shields you from pains. He supplies all your needs, and He guides your feet always. His blessings on you are too numerous to be counted. For if you start counting yourself, you may never finish. May your lips never get tired of exalting Him. May your mouth never be weary of singing His praises. May we never be tired of spreading the news of your great works to the whole world.

PRAYER POINT:
Thank you, Father, for all your blessings towards us. Show us your mercy always, father. Amen.

Day 104

THE INTERCESSION OF THE SPIRIT

*"Likewise the Spirit also helps in our weaknesses.
For we do not know what we should pray for as we
ought, but the Spirit Himself makes intercession
for us with groanings which cannot be uttered."*
-Romans 8:26

When you pray in tongues, you stay strong. But when you are too weak to pray even in words, you need help. And the Lord has provided for this weakness of man. It is a weakness that is caused by our limited mind. It is not of sin but the mind. Every believer needs this help because his mind and flesh limit him and he cannot maximally answer the call to prayer. God cannot wait for us to ask for everything before he does anything. If he has to wait, then we'd be in great trouble because even a lifetime will not be enough to pray for all that needs to be addressed in a year. Our God is love, and He has seen this defect and has provided the ministry of the Holy Spirit in us—our intercessor.

To pray on behalf of a man means that man is not praying for himself at that particular time. Intercession is a prayer made for a man when he is not praying or cannot pray for himself. This means that this particular ministry of the Holy Spirit is not our work. It is the sole duty of the Spirit to pray for us when we are not even aware of it. This is the rest we have in Christ. It means our results in Christ are not entirely dependent on how much we pray for and by ourselves but ultimately by the ministry of the Holy Spirit in us, who prays the very heart of God and does not make a mistake.

Where does this intercession happen? It's in your spirit. It is deep in your spirit and not in your brain. You can't explain it in your dialect; it is a deep thing in your spirit that goes directly from your spirit to God. It does not pass through your mind at all and most of the times, not aware of it. It is our lifeline always. You need to appreciate God for this.

PRAYER POINT:
Thank you, Father, for this wonderful gift of your Holy Spirit In me. What a wonderful thing to know that He prays for me even when I am weak and do not know that I need to pray! I love you, Jesus. Hallelujah!

Day 105

WHEN HE RISES, ENEMIES FLEE

Let God arise, Let His enemies be scattered;
Let those also who hate Him flee before Him.
-Psalms 68:1

Brethren sing praise to the Lord. Let all the earth dance to the rhythm of joy. He is the Alpha and Omega. He is the beginning and the end. No one can stand against him. No one can withstand him. All the powers in heaven and on earth belong to him. He reigns forever. Amen

When God arises to fight your battle, the war is over. The win is on your side. Be glad and happy for you to serve the mighty one. Are you having a hard time, and you think God cannot help you? That sickness has tied you down and had disobeyed all medical treatment. Are all efforts to get that contract which your business needs to survive to be proving abortive? Have you been searching for a job for years now, and nothing has come your way?

Listen! The storm is over. The Lord has arisen. He will fight for you, and you shall hold your peace. All your afflictions are gone. Your sorrows are over. That sickness healed, the job you have been seeking for is yours. The Almighty has secured that contract for you. No need to panic anymore. Your enemies have scattered, for they cannot stand before God. Who can be against you when God is for you? No one. All those who despise God in you will flee before Him.

Sing praises to the Almighty, for he has done great things for you. He is bigger than all your challenges. They are nothing before him. Chant his name everywhere you go.

PRAYER POINT:

Father, I praise your name, for there is none like you. Thank you for all the blessings I have received from you. Thank you for all my battles you fought and the ones you will still fight for me. Amen.

Day 106

THE CALLINGS AND THE GIFTS OF GOD (PART 1)

"I press on toward the goal to win the [supreme and heavenly] prize to which God in Christ Jesus is calling us upward." -Philippians 3:14

God must have called you before you could come to Jesus Christ by faith (John 6:37). When Jesus came into the world as a man, He announced the calling of God into the Kingdom of God and those who believed in Him became part of the Kingdom. The calling of God is first unto repentance to become part of the kingdom, but that's not the end of the calling. The calling of God to you goes beyond the time you received Jesus. That calling is a high calling that you only begin to pursue at salvation. Every believer is called of God to show forth His praise in the earth (1 Peter 2:9). There is a general calling of God unto all men to come into the kingdom, and there is also a personal calling of God unto a particular office, duty, assignment.

You have been made acceptable to God by faith, and so He can now choose you to represent Him especially in the kingdom. Take for illustration, in a company, the board of directors decide on who is to be the CEO, the general manager, and the secretary, etc. to serve the objective of the company at different capacities. However, their offices differ in responsibility and accountability. They are all employees but not with the same appointments. Likewise, in the kingdom of God, we are all believers but not of the same personal callings and responsibilities.

You must find out what you have been called to do particularly in the kingdom. The whole company of believers is to establish the kingdom of God in the earth, but how will that be if there is no division of Labor? For effective work, God has decided in His wisdom to call men and women into diverse duties so that together we can do a whole work without any part missing.

The determination of Paul in Philippian 2:14 was not for the general calling he responded. He was pursuing something higher. Your calling is not just to be a Christian and get to heaven. But you are also to find out your special calling and place in the whole work and labor to do it with all your heart. Are you called to write down the mind of God and send it out to the nations? Are you called to lead the nation or a state in government? Then pursue it and establish a unit of Zion there. Are you called into the fashion world or the technological world? Then be all out. Take the kingdom into the systems. Shut down the works of the devil and give God the praise. You are not here to be a Christian; you are called to affect your world.

I refuse to leave the earth without attaining the high calling of God upon my life. Lord Jesus, reveal by your Holy Spirit your high calling in my life, and I will pursue it. Amen.

Day 107

THE CALLINGS AND THE GIFTS OF GOD (PART 2)

"However, he has given each one of us a special gift according to the generosity of Christ. That is why the scriptures say, 'when he ascended to the height, he led a crowd of captives and gave gifts to his people. '" -Ephesians 4:7-8

The gifts of God are the tools with which a man fulfills his calling and performs his duty in the kingdom. Since the callings of God are supernatural, his gifts also are supernatural. They are for the achievement of the objectives of the Kingdom. God calls a man to duty in the kingdom and then gives him the gifts he needs to perform well in that office. No man will ever be able to do God's work in the earth without God's help.

Because of the natural deficiencies in man, God cannot entrust him with the works of the kingdom without His supernatural way of achieving them. Hence, Jesus Christ seasoned the whole church with the gifts of the Holy Spirit.

By your natural abilities, you cannot do a work that has any eternal value in the kingdom. So Jesus handed over to every one of us a special gift and even many more so that we can do the work of the ministry and to bring edification to the church and to establish the believers in the truth of God's word.

Every gift of God is in accord with His calling. What you don't need you don't have. We all have the diverse manifestation of the gifts of the Spirit as fit for the work we are given to do in the kingdom. This means that we do not need to be envious of any man. What you are gifted to do is quite different from what he is gifted to do. But when you both come together in unity, you both do better work in Jesus's name (Romans 12:4-8).

PRAYER POINT:

Thank you, Jesus, for the gifts you gave unto the church and of which I am a partaker. I thank you father for all the tools you have given to me to do the work of the kingdom, and now I pray that you help me by the Holy Spirit to make use of all that is in me in Christ Jesus. Amen.

Day 108

GOD CALLS TO MAKE

"Everyone who is called by my name, whom I have created for my glory; I have formed him, yes, I have made him." -Isaiah 43:7

Jesus said to Simon and Andrew at the beach, 'follow me, and I will make you fishers of men.' (Matthew 4:19) Halleluiah! Every one that is called of God has been called to be made into what God has prepared for him. There is no man called without a purpose. And the ultimate purpose of every man's calling is to be conformed to the image of Jesus Christ (Romans 8:28-30). There are precision and definition in the heart of God as touching His calling you. You are not part of a company of vagabonds; your calling was deliberate and purposeful. You are not called unto emptiness and wandering. You are called to be made into a wonder. Amen.

Does the name of Christ call you? Then you have been created in glory and for glory. You have been formed to bear His presence. You have been made a habitation of the Holy Ghost. You are not undefined. There is a plan for your life, and God will follow it all through. The high calling of God is a calling into a process—of making you into a useful vessel.

When you were first found as a sinner and saved by grace, you were raw and unrefined. But God cannot do much with that kind of life; He has to bring you into a process whereby He removes things from you and add things to you. He cleanses you and makes you shine brighter both by fire and by water. The process is always difficult as it is for a student to be educated, putting his entire mental faculty to work until he has acquired enough knowledge to be referred to as a literate. But in the end, he can sit amongst the elites of the world because he is now made.

Likewise, as a believer in Jesus's name, you have been called into a process of discipleship—a training by doctrine and experience—until Christ is formed in you. You must not excuse yourself from this. Take corrections and learn as a believer. Your calling is a calling to be made. Amen.

PRAYER POINT:
I submit to the process of making in Jesus's name.

Day 109

GOD CALLS TO SEND

"And he went up on the mountain and called to Him those he himself wanted. And they came to Him. Then He appointed twelve, that they might be with Him and that He might send them out to preach."
-Mark 3:13-14

As you know that God is a God of purpose and intention; he does nothing without reason in His heart. Amen. You now know that God called you to make you. Yes, again, he has called you to send you. After he has made you, he intends to send you out into the world where what he has made you into will be needed. Before you were called, God already knew what He would do with your life in Christ. He already marked out a part for you. And one of the things He planned is to send you out to preach the gospel of the kingdom of God.

Staying with Jesus long enough transforms you into what he looks like, and the design is to send you out in his likeness into the darkness of the world, shining forth the light in you. You are called to become an extension of Christ in the earth.

Whatever God is making out of you is not only for you but also for your community and the world. Can you see the bigger picture? Why you have to go through a rigorous study of the Word now is not just for you to be able to quote scriptures but for nations to be taught the truth with precision and accuracy. Why you have been trained to believe God for divine health and to find out all the scriptures that pertain to healing and health is not just to keep you healthy but to keep diseases out of the nations through the power of God.

There is world-vision in the heart of God. He has not called you to hide you forever. If you think God has only called you so you could be a Christian for yourself and to yourself, you are hindering the move of God in your world.

PRAYER POINT:
I take the power of God inside of me to the world around me in the name of Jesus.

Day 110

FAITHFULNESS IS A DEMAND

"Moreover, it is required in stewards that one be found faithful. But with me it is a very small thing that I should be judged by you or by a human court."-1 Corinthians 4:2-3

Even if everyone else is not faithful, a steward is expected to be faithful with what he has been entrusted with. A steward is one who manages the property or affairs of another man. He is not the owner but a manager and a keeper. As a believer, you are first of all a steward of God's presence. God lives in you, and you must acknowledge that. You have been entrusted with the presence of God in your spirit, and you must be faithful in keeping that presence.

Moreover, you have also been entrusted with some relationships, money, influence, time, knowledge, ideas, and talents; you must be faithful in using all of these to the Glory of God the giver. You are a manager of what belongs to

God, and you will give an account of how you have used all. You must prove yourself worthy of trust.

Faithfulness is keeping the standard, content, form, essence, and focus of a course till the end. It is the ability to see the end of a beginning without losing the passion for the whole thing as it were in the beginning. Faithfulness is watching over what is put in your custody without losing sight of it until the owner appears. Faithfulness is also the relentless working out of a process until the desired result is obtained. Faithfulness is measured with time and pressure. It is the attitude you put on when things are against you, and you are still expected to behave well and coordinated.

Faithfulness is a requirement. It is not a gift. It is work. It is your labor in the power of the Holy Ghost to remain steady in the place of your duty. It doesn't jump at you; you acquire it deliberately. And your faithfulness with little will eventually grant you more from God. The reward of faithful is more trust. As the Lord finds you faithful with the little He has given you today, He trusts you with more tomorrow. Halleluiah!

PRAYER POINT:
I am a faithful believer in the name of Jesus. I labor to keep that which God has entrusted to me by the Holy host in the name of Jesus. When Christ shall return, I will be faithful at my post. Amen.

# Day 111

FAITHFULNESS ATTRACTS
THE ANOINTING

"Therefore, holy brethren, partakers of the heavenly calling, consider the Apostle and High Priest of our confession, Christ Jesus, who was faithful to Him who appointed Him, as Moses also was faithful in all His house." -Hebrews 3:1-2

Jesus remains our ultimate reality and example in the path of glory and excellence. He portrays all we ever will be. He lived a short while on earth, but that was not all about Him. We are called to live a life after His resurrection. However, he was faithful to God in his entire earthly walk. He was obedient in faithfulness and faithful in obedience to God even to the point of death at the cross. He didn't rebel against the will of the Father when it appeared almost inevitable. He preferred to lose His honor than to lose his faithfulness. He kept at it until He entered the greatest glory ever.

How did it happen? It is through faithfulness. Faithfulness is not a gift of the Spirit. It is not by force either. It is a labor of Christian in the power of the Spirit. It is a mix of your decision and the empowerment of the Spirit. It is your choice when you are to choose between contrary options. It is your eternal devotion to God and His Truth, regardless of the consequences.

Because of the faithfulness of Christ he gained a more excellent name (Hebrews 1:4, Philippians 2:8-11, Ephesians 1:21), he was anointed with the oil of gladness (Hebrews 1:9), and he was entrusted with the whole kingdom of heaven and the earth (Hebrews 3:2; Matthew 28:18). Halleluiah!

Faithfulness attracts the anointing for a higher level of kingdom usefulness. Faithfulness widens your area of influence in the world. A faithful man is a friend of God, and he attracts the gifts of God.

PRAYER POINT:
Lord, I submit my will and emotions to the power of the Holy Ghost as I live in this world. And I ask that in your name I will be faithful in all the things of the Kingdom. Amen.

Day 112

THE FIRST FRUIT OF THE KINGDOM (PART 1)

"Now after John was put in prison, Jesus came to Galilee, preaching the gospel of the kingdom of God, and saying, 'the time is fulfilled, and the kingdom of God is at hand. Repent, and believe in the gospel.'"
-Mark 1:14-15

The very first fruit of the kingdom of God is repentance and conviction-repentance from sin and conviction of the gospel. When Jesus started his ministry, he began to preach the kingdom of God. And the first responses he demanded from his hearers were repentance and belief in the words he preached. It was after many have heard Him speak time and again; including the men, he chose as apostles, that he called them to follow him. In the following verses (16 - 20) of our opening scripture, Jesus called Simon, Andrew, James, and John unto Himself and they followed Him immediately. It was not that they were stupid, but they have heard the word of the kingdom over and again, and they were convinced that this Jesus preaching must be the Christ. Before they could leave their businesses to follow a man who only declared he'd make them fishers of men, they must have been convinced of what the Kingdom of God provides.

Without conviction, there is no establishment of the Kingdom in the hearts of men. All other things that follow the kingdom; healing the sick, raising the dead, signs and wonders, and so on, are all to bring men to the point of conviction. Moses kept on showing the signs in Egypt until Pharaoh and the whole of Egypt agreed and were convinced that it was the truth that had demanded the release of Israel. Signs and wonders are purposeful and intentional. All the miracles workable through the name of Jesus are not to have fun but to bring men to the conviction of God's love and acceptance in Christ. Psalm 107 is filled with signs and wonders and their purpose: so that men would praise the LORD for his great love and all his wonderful deeds to them.

PRAYER POINT:

Lord Jesus, I rejoice in you for what you have done and completed for me.

Day 113

THE FIRST FRUIT OF THE KINGDOM (PART 2)

"Then Jesus said to the twelve, "Do you also want to go away?" But Simon Peter answered Him, "Lord, to whom shall we go? You have the words of eternal life. Also, we have come to believe and know that you are the Christ, the Son of the living God." -John 6:67-69

The scripture above reveals that the root of true followership and discipleship is in the conviction of who Jesus is and not in the things he did or the miracles he performed. It came to a time that Jesus began to say the deeper things of the kingdom he had always preached, and it offended many who trooped after him. Because they never had a conviction of His Person in the first place, they withdrew from Jesus. However, the disciples stayed with Him—all through. Your reward in the kingdom is largely dependent on your conviction of the kingdom and its King. Your passion and faithfulness in the business of the kingdom all rest on how deep is your conviction of Jesus Christ. This is the great work of the Holy Spirit in you (John 16:7-13), as allowed by you.

The Holy Spirit convicted you of your godless state while you were yet a sinner and after you were saved, He convinced you of the Truth and now keeps convincing you of the Truth as He guides you into all the revelation of the eternal Truth. However, He can only go as far as you allow Him in the work of convincing you of the truth. To guide is not to force or to manipulate. To guide is to give directives on how to obtain a result or to achieve an aim. The Holy Spirit can only do as much as allowed by you in your readiness to find the truth about any matter in life. Sitting down with the Bible opened before you in a deliberate and purposeful study is a show of your interest in knowing the Truth. But when you never give it a thought to know what the kingdom means and what it does not mean, you also make it known that you are not interested.

Finally, you need to see that all signs and wonders, miracles and manifestations of the Spirit at any point in time are all investments made by God to have a return of the hearts of men.

PRAYER POINT:

I thank you, father, for all the investment you have made so far to bring me into convictions of who Christ is. In Jesus's name, I have the conviction of Christ and His kingdom.

Day 114

THE FIRST FRUIT OF THE KINGDOM (PART 3)

"THAT which was from the beginning, which we have heard, which we have seen with our eyes, which we have looked upon, and our hand have handled, concerning the Word of life—the Life was manifested and we have seen, and bear witness, and declare to you that eternal life which was with the Father and was manifested to us—that which we have seen and have heard we declare unto you..."
-1 John 1:1-3

Apostle John makes it clear in that scripture that they, the apostles, only declare what they have seen, what they have heard, and what they have touched with their hands. They have preached from the place of deep conviction of who Jesus is and what the kingdom is all about. It was not imagination. Halleluiah!

You can only tell others of the Kingdom and Christ to the extent which you have been convinced. Only men of conviction can bring others into conviction. What you do not have, you cannot give. It is the degree of life and energy you have in the gospel that you can release to others as you speak of the Kingdom. To bring men into the kingdom, you must be a witness of the King and the Kingdom.

Now, conviction comes by hearing, seeing, and touching. They are different levels of conviction. You may be convinced by one, two, or three of them. The deepest level of conviction is the one that comes when you hear, see, and touch with your hands the reality of Christ. It becomes eternally alive and impressed in your heart. You cannot deny it anymore. That was the level John was speaking.

At whatever level of conviction, you may be now, seek to hold on to it with all your heart. And labor into deeper levels of convictions. Soak yourself in the truth of the Bible and allow the Holy Spirit to have a free course in your life. Through diverse experiences, circumstances, revelation, and challenges, He will guide you into a deeper conviction of Christ and His Lordship.

The words of eternal life can be heard, seen, and touched. Raising the dead is one way of handling the words of eternal life. Preaching the gospel and seeing nations turn to God is one of seeing the words of eternal life. You can do business with the words of eternal life until you are entirely consumed by its reality. Amen.

PRAYER POINT:
I hear, and I see and I touch the Word of Eternal life in Jesus's name. Amen.

Day 115

HEAL THE SICK (PART 1)

"And when He had called His twelve disciples to Him, He gave them power over unclean spirits, to cast them out, and to heal all kinds of disease ...And as you go, preach, saying, 'the Kingdom of heaven is at hand.' Heal the sick... " -Matthew 10:1, 7, 8

Once the Kingdom of Heaven is preached, the unclean spirits are in trouble. Halleluiah! When Jesus would send out His disciples for fieldwork after a few years of training, he sent them with a share of the power He carried in him. And he commanded them to cast out unclean spirits and to heal all manners of sickness and all manners of diseases. Amen.

There is a progression here. Before the kingdom of God could be established in the earth, the kingdom of heaven must come into the earth. The Kingdom of God is the portion of God in the earth—the church. It is the kingdom of Christ and his people; a fraction of the earth. The kingdom of God is what came about when God left heaven and came into the earth to rule amongst humanity. The

Kingdom of God is not equal to the kingdom of heaven; it is only an extension of the kingdom of heaven.

The kingdom of God is that kingdom into which everyone who believes in Christ comes. And by extension, he partakes in the Kingdom of heaven. The Kingdom of God has its palace and throne in the earth—in the heart of man. But the kingdom of heaven has its throne in heaven. The kingdom of heaven is the eternal sum of all the realms in heaven and on the earth and even in hell where the will of God overrules—the realms of the angels, of man (believers and nonbelievers) and demons. Why you need this understanding is for you to know why it was the preaching of the kingdom of heaven that precedes the healing of the sick.

When the Kingdom of heaven is being preached, all things are brought under the supreme authority in time and eternity. At that point, all demons must leave as they are told. No jurisdiction is left to the devil. It is an inheritance issue; it is a dominion issue. Halleluiah! All manners of diseases are healed, and the chains of darkness are broken without any reserve. It is the superimposition of heaven literally on the earth. It is not that God leaves heaven to come into the earth. Heaven itself comes with all its citizens and workforces. It is not a portion of the church but of all that is in heaven. In that kind of atmosphere, nothing is impossible. Thousands of dead men can rise; a million sick people can be healed at once as they are immersed in heaven on earth. Halleluiah!

PRAYER POINT:
I am a child of God, and I am part of both the kingdom of God and Heaven. I walk in the power of the Kingdom and God and of Heaven in the name of Jesus.

HEAL THE SICK (PART 2)

"But if I cast out demons with the finger of God, surely the Kingdom of God has come upon you."
-Luke 11:20

Having understood the link between the preaching of the Kingdom of Heaven and the healing of the sick, you will now see the link between the casting out of demons and healing the sick.

When the Kingdom of heaven is superimposed on the kingdom of the earth, demons are bound to come out of their hiding places. When this happens, afflictions are stopped, and diseases are cured. Unclean spirits cause unclean experiences of man. All sicknesses and diseases—known and unknown; named and unnamed—have their first roots in the dark kingdom and could be traced to their first roots; just as death and sin are of darkness. God never created man with sickness and disease and so they came with the fall of man in sin and death. Every sickness leads ultimately to death. And this is not of heaven and it is not of God.

In the light of this truth, more sicknesses and diseases will be healed when their roots in darkness have been destroyed and the demons are cast out in Jesus's name (Mark 16:17-18). If demons are cast out of the body, the body is then free to accept the health God gives to man abundantly.

PRAYER POINT:

In the name of Jesus, I cast out devils and I heal the sick. I heal the sick. I heal all manners of sicknesses and all manners of diseases. With God and the power in the name of Jesus, no sickness is incurable to me. I cast out the unclean spirit and set men free from their afflictions in the name of Jesus. Amen.

*D*ay *117*

ESTABLISHING THE KINGDOM OF GOD

"For the kingdom of God does not consist in talk but in power." *-1 Corinthians 4:20*

To establish the kingdom of God in a place means it was not there before. And to bring it there, you must preach the kingdom of heaven. You have understood from the last teaching that the kingdom of heaven is larger than the church. It covers the whole realm of existence. Halleluiah! When you enter a place where the kingdom of God was not, it is sure that the kingdom of darkness is in charge of that place. And to establish the kingdom of God, you will first need to destroy the kingdom of darkness and chase them out of place. But this must be in the power of the Kingdom of Heaven and not just in mere talks.

At the entrance of the Kingdom of Heaven in that place, strongholds of Satan are pulled down, evil trees are uprooted, structures raised unto demons are broken down, and altars are defied (Jeremiah 1:9-10). Not until the Kingdom Of heaven has overruled the kingdom of darkness through the Word of His power, and manifestations of the Holy Ghost, you cannot establish the Kingdom of God in the place. Until the power of God hits down every power of darkness that has put people in captivities, the kingdom of God cannot be established. Much talk without much power has no good to do with men. It is like a man using a blunt ax to cut down a very large tree; he may spend eternity doing that.

It becomes a labor of foolishness to go into a land, to establish the kingdom of God without= understanding the kingdom of heaven and the gospel of the kingdom. Jesus himself makes it clear in Mark 3:27, that 'No one can enter a strong man's house and plunder his goods unless he first binds the strong man. And then he will plunder his house.' You must approach darkness in the power of Light in heaven. You must speak from a place of authority in heaven. Amen.

PRAYER POINT:

I thank you father of all spirits and of all flesh, for you are King over all realms and have put all things under the feet of Jesus Christ our Lord. I am in Christ and I preach the kingdom in the power of the Holy Ghost. I am not talkative but I am full of the manifestations of the Spirit to destroy the manifestations of darkness in Jesus's name. Amen.

<h1 style="text-align:center">Day 118</h1>

OLD THINGS ARE PASSED AWAY

"Therefore if any man be in Christ, he is a new creation: old things are passed away; behold, all things become new." -2 Corinthians 5:17

You must not allow your past to trouble your present. No matter what you have done or what has happened in the past, your present matters more. God is more interested in your present and your future. The past has passed! If you have been swimming in sins before, now that you have resolved to flee from evil, you are now a new creation. Old things including your sins, have passed away, and all things become new.

God is not a man. Unlike man, God forgives and forgets our offenses. He will never recall them. When God looks at you, He sees that whatever might have been wrong in your life before you were born again is now passed away. You may not "feel" or think so, but that doesn't negate His truth. Besides, that's the reason He told you (2 Corinthians 5:17) because you couldn't know any other way, except through the Word. So now, you're to act on His Word.

If it's true that old things are passed away, then it means you can't have "inherited curses" or an inherited sickness or disease. There couldn't be such a thing as a generational curse, because you are now a new species—a new creation!

PRAYER POINT:

Lord, course my old life to pass away and please give me the grace to start living a new life in you as a new creation.

Day 119

THROUGH YOU, HIS LIGHT SHINES

The spirit of a man is the lamp of the Lord,
searching all the inner depths of his heart.
-Proverbs 20:27

Did you read the Bible verse above?
"Hold on. Do not go any further. Go back and read it again".
Have you? Then think about it. Read again and give it some more thoughts. What do you understand? This verse is profound, so deep that its meaning gladdens my heart.

God, through you, shows the world his heart. You are God's intentions. The innermost thoughts of God are portrayed through an instrument, which is you. Amazing right? Hold on, does your action portray what God wants? Do people look at you and say, yes, this is truly a child of God? Do you live your life as a true believer of God?

I understand how difficult life can be. Sometimes it leaves you weary and sad, that you will be tempted to throw in-the-go towel, leave the difficult narrow part and tread the easier wide road. More so how difficult it is to be a true believer in this 21st century. With technology, temptations are all over us. But giving up is not an option.

Jesus is telling you today that all his thoughts, all the things he wants people of the world to know he can portray through you. He is saying that you are a mirror through which the world sees his image.

PRAYER POINT:
Dear Lord, I apologize for all the times through the actions I passed across wrong messages to the world. Grant me the grace to live my life not as I want but as it pleases only you. Amen.

Day 120

GOD GOES AHEAD OF YOU

"Yet, for all that, you did not believe the LORD your God, who went in the way before you to search out a place to pitch your tents, to show you the way you should go, in the fire by night and in the clouds by day." -Deuteronomy 1:32-33

Again, what the Lord does for you as He goes ahead of you is to find a place of rest for you. It is like a shepherd going before his flock, leading them to a place of rest and peace from all predators. You don't know what is ahead of you but God knows all. You don't know what awaits you, but God knows all. Because of infinite knowledge and eternal love for you, He goes ahead of you, seeking a place for you to establish yourself and enlarge your coast. Can you see how much He loves you?

Every good father wants to secure a good future for his children. As a child of God and an obedient one at that, your Father in Heaven has gone ahead of you in time, through your future, and has decided to find a place of rest for you. Isn't it wonderful? It means you are not a vagabond in this world. You may not have an earthly parent anymore, but God will still establish you. You may not have many helpers to help you lift your burdens, but Jesus has offered you a hand, and you can trust Him. You may lack many things other youths have because of your background or because of some experienced you have had in the past, must you must see how God is going ahead of you now to find your place for you and make you established.

In Matthew 11:28, Jesus offers you a call today,

"Come unto me, all you who labor and are heavy-laden and overburdened and I will cause you to rest. [I will ease and relieve and refresh your souls.]" (The Message version)

Only the Lord Jesus Christ the place of true rest for your soul. Having many friends or more money will not give you the kind of rest and peace He offers you today. Will you take what He offers and allow Him to lead you as a shepherd leads His sheep from rest to rest?

PRAYER POINT:

Christ Jesus, my good shepherd, I thank you for the wonderful plan you have for me in this world. I believe you know the place of true rest for me in this life; now I ask that you hold my hand and lead me on out of every storm into rest and establish me. Also, enlarge my coast and influence for your kingdom in Jesus's name. Amen.